Susan Grant

Cambridge IGCSE® and O Level

Economics

Workbook

CAMBRIDGE
UNIVERSITY PRESS

CAMBRIDGE
UNIVERSITY PRESS

University Printing House, Cambridge CB2 8BS, United Kingdom

One Liberty Plaza, 20th Floor, New York, NY 10006, USA

477 Williamstown Road, Port Melbourne, VIC 3207, Australia

314–321, 3rd Floor, Plot 3, Splendor Forum, Jasola District Centre, New Delhi – 110025, India

79 Anson Road, #06–04/06, Singapore 079906

Cambridge University Press is part of the University of Cambridge.

It furthers the University's mission by disseminating knowledge in the pursuit of education, learning and research at the highest international levels of excellence.

Information on this title: www.cambridge.org/ 9781108440400

First published 2018

20 19 18 17 16 15 14 13 12 11

Printed in Malaysia by Vivar Printing

A catalogue record for this publication is available from the British Library

ISBN 978-1-108-44040-0 Paperback

....

iii

This workbook complements the IGCSE and O Level Economics coursebook and aims to help you consolidate your economics knowledge and understanding and develop the skills of analysis and evaluation.

The workbook has been designed as a flexible resource to support you on your economics skills journey. The questions are designed to provide further opportunities for you to check your ability to provide solutions to a variety of economics problems and practise your economics skills.

Learning summary

Before completing the activities in this section, review your work on these topics:

- The nature of the economic problem
- Factors of production
- Opportunity cost
- Production possibility curves

Learning summary
a summary list that briefly sets out the learning aims for each section, helping students with navigation of the content.

Link
highlights where to find further information on key topics in each section in the Coursebook.

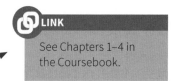

LINK

See Chapters 1–4 in the Coursebook.

20 More money may flow from _____ countries to _____ countries if debt repayments are greater than foreign aid.

Stretch content
A blue line in the margin has been added to identify areas of stretch content that go beyond the syllabus. You will not be expected to know and learn these for your course, but you may want to use them to challenge yourself further, and in some cases they may help you to better understand a concept you are learning.

TIP
First consider what relationship you would expect to find between the consumption of tea and the supply of milk. Then examine whether the data supports this expected relationship.

Tip
provides additional context, reminders or useful information to complement the main text.

Answering four-part question 2

Below is a sample answer to question 2. The answer contains some common weaknesses. Read each part and consider how the answer could be improved.

a Equilibrium price is the price that consumers are prepared to pay.

b A rise in demand will shift the demand curve to the right. This will cause price to fall and supply to extend as shown in the diagram.

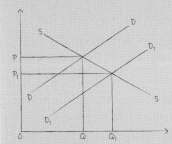

c There are a number of factors that influence the price elasticity of demand. One is price. The higher the price, the lower the demand. Income is an important influence. A rise in income will increase demand for most goods, that is normal goods. Demand for inferior goods would fall. Changes in the price of substitutes and complements are another influence. A rise in the price of a substitute will cause consumers to buy more of this product. A fall in the price of a complement would also increase demand for the product.

d PED figures are a useful source of information. If PED is greater than 1, it means that demand is elastic. In this case, a producer could raise revenue by lowering price. The producer should not raise price as demand will fall.

- If PED is less than 1, it means demand is inelastic. This time, a producer could increase revenue by raising price. It should not lower price as this will lower revenue.

- If PED is 1, it is unity, a change in price will have no effect. If the firm raises or lowers price, revenue will remain the same.

- PED figures are very useful to a producer as it lets him know what effect a change in price will have on revenue. Firms want to earn revenue as the more revenue they have compared to their costs, the more profit they will have.

Answering four-part questions
provides an example answer to a four-part question, highlighting common weaknesses that enable students to reflect on how the answer could be improved.

Improve the answer
suggestions on how to improve an example answer to a four-part question.

Improve the answer...

Here are some ways to improve the above answer. Did you think about these?

a This is an incomplete answer. It is only considering the demand side and only part of the demand side as demand depends not just on what consumers are prepared to pay but also on what they are willing to pay.

b It would have been useful to have used a ruler in drawing the diagram and the axes should have been labelled. The most significant weakness here is that the student has drawn the demand and supply curves round the wrong way. The demand curve the student has drawn is actually the supply curve and the supply curve is the demand curve! This confusion leads the student into confused thinking as an increase in demand will cause price to rise. It is a rise in price which results in an extension in supply.

c The student has made a relatively common mistake, that is confused the factors that influence PED for a product with the factors that influence demand for a product.

d There are three weaknesses with this answer. One is that the points are not always fully established. For example, the student writes 'In this case, a producer could raise revenue by lowering price' but does not explain why. The candidate also writes 'The producer should not raise price as demand will fall.' This statement does not distinguish between elastic demand and perfectly inelastic demand as the inverse relationship occurs in both cases. Another weakness is that the student does not apply PED to a particular brand of smartphones as required by the question. The last weakness is that the answer does not evaluate as it only considers why PED figures may be a useful source of information and not why they might not be.

Introduction

This Workbook is designed to help you develop your understanding of economics, to build up your skills and to enable you to assess your progress.

The book can be used in conjunction with the Cambridge IGCSE and O Level Economics textbook I have written. The book starts by exploring how you can develop the skills of an economist that you will need to be proficient in. It is then divided into six sections which correspond to the sections of the syllabus and the textbook. Each section, in turn, is divided into ten parts.

The first part asks you to match terms with the appropriate definitions. Some of the terms and definitions are quite similar so you need to take care. Undertaking this exercise should reinforce your knowledge of the terms and emphasise to you the need for precision.

In the second part, you have to fill in missing words. This requires you to process what you have learned to find words that ensure the sentences make economic sense and to help you build up links between, for example, causes and effects.

One of the skills an economist needs is the ability to undertake calculations. The third part provides you with the opportunity to build up your numerical skills.

Parts 4 and 5 focus on two other skills of an economist. These are the ability to interpret and draw diagrams. The diagrams selected are the key ones associated with the different sections of the syllabus.

Part 6 will help you to both check your understanding and to develop your multiple choice technique. You will find a total of 170 multiple choice questions in the book.

In Part 7 you can practise your ability to process and interpret economic terms by identifying the similarities and differences between terms.

Part 8 encourages you to produce longer answers and gives you the opportunity to interpret economic information and apply your knowledge to current, real world issues.

Part 9 provides four-part questions which require longer written answers. These seek to develop the key skill of writing in a logical and lucid manner.

Finally, Part 10 offers guidance to help you develop strong responses to four-part questions.

You can tackle a section of the book once you have completed the corresponding section of your course, or you can choose to work through all the sections towards the end of your course.

As with the accompanying textbook, this book seeks to cover all the topics in the syllabus and to provide you with additional concepts to strengthen your understanding and the quality of the answers you can provide. These additional concepts are:

- Absolute and comparative advantage
- Aggregate demand and aggregate supply analysis
- Allocative and productive efficiency
- Average propensity to consume and average propensity to save
- Cost benefit analysis
- Foreign aid

The figures in the book shown as $s are US dollars.

I hope you find the tasks in this book both interesting and useful. Studying economics can be fascinating and can provide benefits both to you and to society. Alfred Marshall, a famous British economist, wrote in 1885 that his objective was to send economists "out into the world with cool heads but warm hearts, willing to give some at least of their best to grappling with the suffering around them; resolved not to rest content till they have done what in them lies to discover how far it is possible to open up to all the material means of a refined and noble life." Much has happened since Marshall wrote this, but still it remains a worthy objective.

In preparing this new edition, I would like to thank my editor, Susan Ross, for her very useful suggestions and help. All sample answers have been written by the author.

Susan Grant

Developing skills

The skills of an economist

Economists use a range of tools and skills to interpret economic issues and events, to explain these and to make recommendations on choices and policy measures. Whilst studying Economics, you will develop a number of these skills including the ability to:

- show knowledge and understanding of the subject
- interpret and draw diagrams
- interpret data which may be in the form of written information, statistical tables, diagrams and graphs
- undertake basic calculations
- use economic formulas and equations
- analyse economic issues and events
- evaluate economic choices and policy measures
- write in a clear manner, using economic concepts and terms.

The skills you will need

This section will help you develop the key skills of an economist. It supports the Cambridge IGCSE/O Level Economics syllabus. The skills of an economist can be divided into three broad categories). These are:

Knowledge and understanding

Students should be able to:

- show knowledge and understanding of economic definitions, formulas, concepts and theories
- use economic terminology.

Analysis

Students should be able to:

- select, organise and interpret data
- use economic information and data to recognise patterns and to deduce relationships
- apply economic analysis to written, numerical, diagrammatic and graphical data
- analyse economic issues and situations, identifying and developing links.

Evaluation

Students should be able to:

- evaluate economic information and data
- distinguish between economic analysis and increased statements
- recognise that economic thinking has limits and uncertainties
- assess alternative outcomes of possible economics decisions and events
- communicate economic thinking in a logical manner.
- Source of `Knowledge and understanding', `Analysis' and `Evaluation': Cambridge Assessment International Examinations IGCSE/O Level syllabus

Showing knowledge and understanding

Knowledge and understanding of economic terms, concepts and topics is the first skill developed. It underpins analysis and evaluation. You cannot analyse or evaluate something until you know and understand it. You will not be familiar with some of the terms in economics but the more you use them, the more confident you will become.

Interpreting diagrams

Diagrams have to be considered carefully. Check to see what is being shown on the axes. The vertical axis is the line that runs up and down and is sometimes referred to as the *y* axis. The horizontal axis, also called the *x* axis, runs from side to side.

Then check what is plotted on the diagram. Figure 1 shows how many chocolate bars firms are willing and able to sell at different prices. The line which plots the different quantities that firms will supply at different prices is known as a supply curve. The diagram shows that firms are willing and able to supply more chocolate bars, the higher the price. Economic theory supports this relationship. This is because a higher price is likely to increase the revenue that the firm will receive.

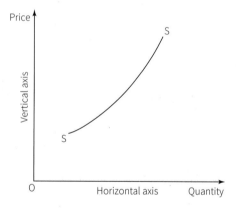

Figure 1: A supply curve showing how many chocolate bars firms are willing and able to sell at different prices

Drawing diagrams

Diagrams are a key tool of an economist. They are used to analyse theories, predictions and relationships.

The main types of diagrams you may be required to draw are a demand and supply diagram, a production possibility diagram, cost curve diagrams and revenue diagrams. Although aggregate demand and supply diagrams are not on the syllabus, they can be used to explain, analyse and evaluate macroeconomic issues and policies.

When drawing a diagram, it is important that you:

- use a ruler to draw the axes
- label the axes clearly and accurately
- label the curves accurately
- make sure the diagram is large enough to be seen clearly
- where appropriate, explain what the diagram shows.

Interpreting data

Written data

Over your course, you will come across a variety of forms of written data. These are likely to include passages from textbooks, newspaper articles, website articles and examination-style questions.

It is often useful to read through written data quickly the first time and then go back to read it more carefully.

Statistical tables

Statistical tables can be used to show and analyse changes in economic data and economic relationships, and to make comparisons between, for example, the behaviour of different households, firms and countries.

Table 1 shows data of the number of cans that a firm has estimated it would be able to sell in a day at different prices. For example, it has estimated that it would be able to sell 30 cans if it charged $1, but only 20 cans if the price is $1.6.

Table 1: Number of cans of a soft drink that would be sold per day at different prices

Price of a can of soft drink ($)	Number of cans of soft drink that would be sold in a day
1.0	30
1.2	28
1.4	25
1.6	20
1.8	12
2.0	2

TIP

Throughout this section, there are questions to help you develop the full range of skills that you will need in order to successfully start thinking like an economist. You may wish to answer these as you encounter them, or to wait until you feel fully prepared.

Question 1: Using Table 1, is the relationship between the price of the can and the number of cans sold the one you would expect? Explain your answer.

Interpreting graphs

As with diagrams, it is important to check the axes carefully. They may be showing absolute figures or relative figures. For example, the vertical axis may be showing wage rates in dollars (absolute) or an index of wage rates (relative).

A graph may also be showing absolute figures or changes in those figures over time. For example, a graph may show a firm's total cost in different years or the change in its total cost over a period of time. Figure 2 below shows the percentage change in a firm's total cost over a period of five years. Figure 3 shows the percentage change in a country's price level (the average of prices of goods and services in an economy) over the same period.

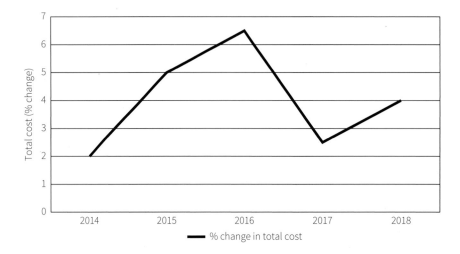

Figure 2: Percentage change in a firm's total cost, 2014–2018

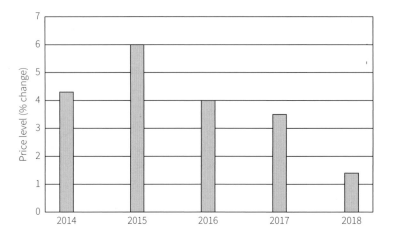

Figure 3: Percentage change in a country's price level, 2014–2018

Question 2:

a Using Figure 2, explain what happened to the firm's total cost over the period shown.

b Using Figure 3, explain in which year the price level was highest.

Types of graphs

Economists make use of a wide range of graphs.

Time series line graphs

A time series line graph is commonly used. It plots one, or more, series of figures over a period of time. Figure 2 is an example of a time series line graph. A time series line graph may show trends. Figure 4, for example, shows that while the number of economics students in a school had an upward trend over the period 2014 to 2018, the number of geography students had a downward trend.

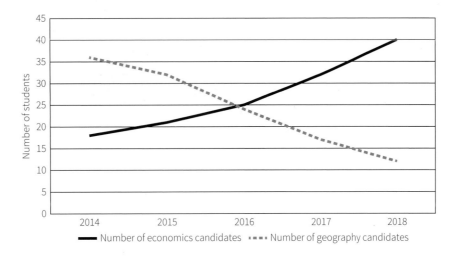

Figure 4: A school's economics and geography students, 2014–2018

Bar charts

Bar charts, such as Figure 3, show one or more bars either vertically or horizontally. The bars are used to compare data over a period of time or between different economic variables. The larger the height (in the case of vertical columns) or length (in the case of horizontal axes), the greater the magnitude of the data. Figure 5 compares the number of people and the number of cars they have in each house in a street.

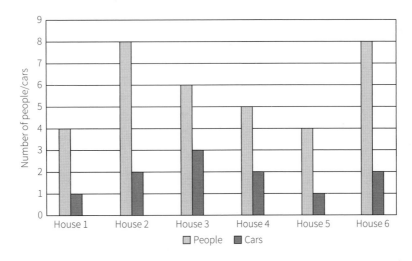

Figure 5: The number of people living in each house in a street and the number of cars owned by the occupants of each house

Pie charts

Pie charts are circular diagrams that are divided into segments usually showing percentages. Figure 6 shows how a person spends a day.

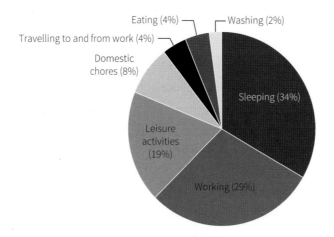

Figure 6: Use of hours in a day

Question 3: Using Figure 6, compare the time the person spends on leisure activities, sleeping and working.

Scatter diagrams

A scatter diagram is used to see if there is a relationship between two variables. If there could be a line of best fit between the pair of variables that is upward sloping from left to right, it suggests a positive relationship between the two, with both moving in the same direction. If, on the other hand, there could be a downward sloping line of best fit, there may a negative relationship, with the variables moving in opposite directions. Of course, it is possible that the pair of variables may be scattered randomly on the graph. This would indicate no relationship between the two variables. Figure 7 shows the hours students spend on revising, on average, per week and their success rates in passing examinations with 0% indicating that they had failed all their subjects and 100% indicating that they had passed all their exams.

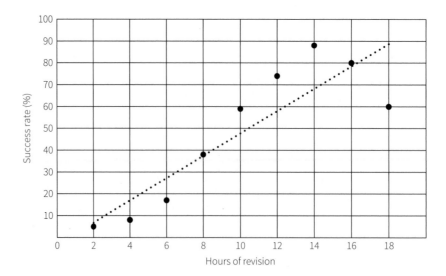

Figure 7: Success rate

Question 4: Comment on the relationship shown in Figure 7.

Undertaking basic calculations

Economists interpret numerical data and undertake calculations. The numerical data that you might be expected to interpret could include index numbers, percentages and averages. The calculations could also include percentages, averages, multiplication, division, addition and subtraction.

It is important that you do not get confused between units, tens, hundreds, thousands, millions, billions and trillions – see Table 2.

Table 2: Different sizes of numbers

Number		Number of 0s
One	1	0
Ten	10	1
Hundred	100	2
Thousand	1000	3
Million	1 000 000	6
Billion	1 000 000 000	9
Trillion	1 000 000 000 000	12

Question 5: Complete the following calculations:

a   If five firms sell a product at $40, $45, $48, $50 and $57, what is the average price charged?

b   60% of the 30 students in class A buy an economics textbook and 50% of the 40 students in class B buy the book. What is the difference in the number of textbooks the two classes buy?

c   A football club played 40 matches. It won 22 and drew 13. What percentage did it lose?

d   A country has a total income of $500 billion (bn) and a population of 20 million (m). What is the income per head of the population (average income)?

Using economic formulas and equations

A good economist needs to be familiar with a number of formulas and equations, such as: price elasticity of demand, price elasticity of supply, average total cost, average fixed cost, average variable cost, average revenue and real GDP per head.

Analysing economic issues and events

Analysis is built on knowledge and understanding. It involves explaining points, establishing links between points, applying economic concepts, interpreting data, making use of diagrams and undertaking calculations.

The key words to bear in mind when you are seeking to establish analysis are 'why' and 'how'. For example, if you are asked to analyse the causes of a fall in the death rate and you identify an improvement in nutrition you need to explain why this could have resulted in people living longer.

As you progress through your course, you will start to think like an economist. This involves thinking logically, analysing key economic issues, and considering causes and consequences. You will learn to apply economic theory and concepts to new situations. One of the reasons why economics is highly regarded as an academic subject is because it develops the skill to think in a clear and reasoned way.

Evaluating economic choices and policy measures

This is the highest order skill. It builds on both knowledge and understanding and analysis. It involves assessing, for example, both sides of an argument, costs and benefits, possible different outcomes of a choice and the effectiveness of different government policy measures. A professional economist working for a government, for example, may be asked to draw up the case both for raising the standard rate of income tax and for leaving it unchanged, and to explain which she would recommend. An economist working for a firm may be required to assess the advantages and disadvantages for the firm resulting from the introduction of a national minimum wage.

TIP

The most influential economists tend to be those who can write clearly. It is important that you write clearly so you can display your knowledge and understanding of the subject, and show you can use economic concepts and terms to analyse and evaluate economic issues.

Help to prepare for examination

There are two papers:

*   Paper 1 is a multiple choice question paper.
*   Paper 2 is a structured question paper designed to measure knowledge and understanding, analysis and evaluation.

    The paper is structured into two sections. Section A consists of a compulsory data response question; whilst section B contains multiple four-part questions.

Question 6: Match each command word with an appropriate definition.

Command word		Definition	
1	Analyse	**a**	Write about issue(s) or topic(s) in depth in a structured way.
2	Calculate	**b**	Express in clear terms.
3	Define	**c**	Name/select/recognise.
4	Describe	**d**	Provide an answer from a given source or recall/memory.
5	Discuss	**e**	Examine in detail to show meaning, identify elements and the relationship between them.
6	Explain	**f**	State the points of a topic, give characteristics and main factors.
7	Give	**g**	Set out purposes or reasons, make the relationship between things evident, provide why and/or how, and support with relevant evidence.
8	Identify	**h**	Work out from given facts, figures or information.
9	State	**i**	Give precise meaning.

Source of command words and definitions: Cambridge Assessment International Education IGCSE/O Level syllabus

Examples of different quality responses

The table below shows a variety of different quality responses to the following question. All sample responses have been written by the author.

Discuss whether or not the introduction of supply-side policy measures would lower a high rate of inflation.

Sample answer	Comments
Supply-side policy measures may or may not lower a high rate of inflation.	This sentence essentially repeats the question
Supply-side policy measures include government spending on education and training, cuts in income tax and corporation tax, cuts in unemployment benefit and privatisation.	This sentence shows an understanding of the nature of supply-side policy measures.
Increased government spending on education and training may raise the skills of workers. This may increase labour productivity which can lower costs of production and increase productivity potential. The higher total supply will reduce cost-push inflation. Lower direct taxes and lower unemployment benefit may increase the incentive to work and innovate. These measures can, again, increase total supply. If total supply rises in line with any increase in total demand, the price level will not increase. Privatisation may reduce cost-push inflation if the industries affected operate more efficiently in the private sector. This may occur if the industries are broken up into different firms to create competition.	These paragraphs analyse a number of policy measures. Links are provided between the policy measures and a lower inflation rate.

Supply–side policy measures have the potential to lower inflation by increasing total supply. There are, however, a number of reasons why they may not be successful. If the inflation rate is high, workers, firms and households may expect the price level to continue to rise at a high rate. This may mean that, even if they are more skilled, labour costs may not fall as workers will press for higher wages. Firms may raise their prices in anticipation that their costs of production will continue to rise. Households may still buy, for example, furniture, in the expectation that prices will be higher in the future. There is no guarantee that supply–side policy measures will work. For example, workers may respond to a cut in income tax by working fewer hours rather than more hours. They may value leisure time more highly than a rise in earnings. Firms in the private sector may be less efficient than those in the public sector, especially if they gain monopoly power by merging with and eliminating rivals. Some supply–side policy measures also take time to have an effect. For example, more government spending on education may take ten or more years to have an effect.	This answer is exploring both sides of the argument in some depth. The comments are clear and lucid.

How the Workbook may help you develop and assess your skills

Part 1 Definitions

Matching terms and definitions can help you to check your knowledge of the key terms, some of which might seem quite similar. Even at this stage, you might be able to work out which definitions go with which terms.

Question 7: Match each term with an appropriate definition.

1	Microeconomic policies	a	A government's objectives for the whole economy
2	Regulation	b	A steady rise in the general price level
3	Macroeconomic policies	c	Policies designed to influence the whole economy
4	Stable inflation	d	Rules and laws

Part 2 Missing words

This activity tests both your knowledge and understanding and helps you see some links.

Question 8: Fill in the missing words.

1   Paper 1 consists of _____ multiple choice questions and tests _____ and _____.

2   Section 4 of the syllabus is _____ _____ _____ _____ and includes fiscal policy, monetary policy and _____ policy.

3   Knowledge and understanding is demonstrated by providing _____ definitions and analysis by providing _____ between points.

Part 3 Calculations

Carrying out calculations is one of the key skills of an economist. The questions in this part of each section of the Workbook will provide you with the opportunity to undertake some of the most common types of calculation you will encounter in your course.

Part 4 Interpreting diagrams

This is a useful skill, It will increase your ability to use diagrams in an appropriate way when answering questions.

You may want to attempt Question 9 when you have covered production possibility curves.

xvii

Question 9: Analyse what Figure 8 shows.

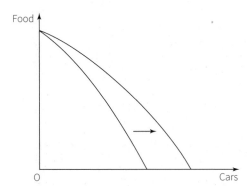

Figure 8

Part 5 Drawing diagrams

This Workbook will provide you with plenty of opportunity to draw and apply diagrams. It will also help you to integrate the diagrams you draw into your written answers.

Part 6 Multiple choice questions

The questions below will help you to familiarise yourself with Multiple Choice Questions and how they are often set out.

Question 10: Answer the five multiple choice questions.

1 A government sets a maximum price on rented accommodation above the equilibrium price. What will be the likely outcome?

    A An unofficial market in rented accommodation will develop

    B Rents will remain unchanged

    C Landlords will provide more rented accommodation

    D Some potential tenants will be unable to find accommodation

2 What is meant by deregulation?

    A The imposition of price controls

    B The imposition of taxes

    C The removal of competition

    D The removing of rules and laws

3 Which factor may stop economic growth?

    A Automatic stabilisers

    B A lack of skilled labour

    C A large multiplier effect

    D A rise in net exports

4 Which is the most accurate measure of living standards?

    A GDP

    B GDP per head

    C Real GDP

    D Real GDP per head

5 Why may an increase in GDP be accompanied by a decrease in living standards?

    A Illiteracy may have decreased

    B Negative externalities may have increased

    C The population may have decreased

    D Working conditions may have improved

Part 7 Similarities and differences

These parts test your ability to apply your knowledge and understanding and should help you avoid confusion between similar terms.

Part 8 Data response questions

These questions provide you with the opportunity to apply your knowledge and understanding to questions based on real world issues and events. You will receive some guidance on answering these questions in the Workbook. As you work through the course and gain more confidence and experience, the amount of guidance is reduced.

Answering data response questions comes close to what some professional economists do, that is interpret economic data and report on it. Data response questions have the advantage that they can assess all the skills. Question 11 shows a shortened example of a data response question.

Source material: Milan and Paris tackle congestion

The city of Milan in Italy has a congestion charge on motorists wanting to enter the centre of the city. The intention is to reduce traffic and so reduce traffic time and pollution.

The charges are levied on a sliding scale of engine types, with the most polluting vehicles being charged the most and the least polluting ones, such as scooters and electric cars, being exempt. The charge applies on weekdays from 7.30 am to 7.30 pm. Residents can pay a fixed annual fee or buy discounted multiple entry passes. The scheme raises revenue, two-thirds of which is used to subsidise public transport.

In 2016, the French government banned old cars from the streets of Paris from Monday to Friday. Figure 9 compares the number of new passenger cars on the roads in selected countries and the growth in population of those countries.

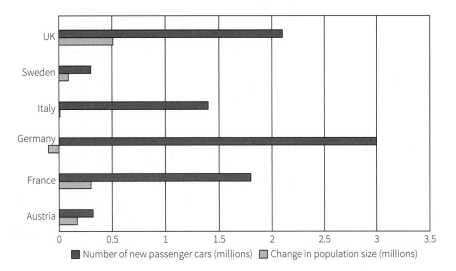

Figure 9: Change in population size and number of new passenger cars in selected European countries, 2016

Question 11: Referring to the source material in your responses, complete all parts of Question 11.

a   Identify an external cost caused by traffic congestion.   **[1]**
b   Explain how a congestion charge can reduce travel time for motorists.   **[2]**
c   Explain why a congestion charge may not apply at night.   **[4]**

d Analyse, using Figure 9, the relationship between changes in population and the number of new passenger cars on the road.　　　　　　　　**[4]**

e Analyse, using a demand and supply diagram, how a subsidy given to bus companies would affect the market for bus travel.　　　　　　　　**[5]**

f Discuss whether or not the congestion charge in Milan will reduce the output of car producers in Italy.　　　　　　　　**[6]**

Part 9 Four-part questions

The Workbook provides you with plenty of opportunity to answer this type of question. As with the data response questions, you will receive some guidance in answering the questions. As you work through the Workbook and gain more confidence and experience, the amount of guidance is reduced.

Question 12

Put these questions on inflation into the order in which they would appear in a four-part question:

1 Explain the difference between demand-pull inflation and cost-push inflation.

2 Define *inflation*.

3 Discuss whether or not a reduction in a country's inflation rate will reduce its unemployment rate.

4 Analyse how an increase in the rate of income tax could reduce inflation.

Learning summary

Before completing the activities in this section, review your work on these topics:

- The nature of the economic problem
- Factors of production
- Opportunity cost
- Production possibility curves

LINK

See Chapters 1–4 in the Coursebook.

Part 1 Definitions

The activity below is designed to check your knowledge and understanding of some of the key terms used in this section.

Match the following terms with an appropriate definition. For example, if you think an 'inability of workers to change jobs and location' defines 'scarcity', match 1 with c. Each term has an appropriate definition. If you find that you are left with a term and a definition which do not appear to match, you should review your other matches.

1	Scarcity	a	Natural resources
2	The economic problem	b	Economic resources
3	Wants	c	Inability of workers to change jobs and location
4	Land	d	Inability to produce everything that people want
5	Capital	e	Products that have an opportunity cost
6	Labour immobility	f	Products that do not have an opportunity cost
7	Factors of production	g	Products people desire to have
8	Opportunity cost	h	Human made resources
9	Economic goods	i	An insufficient quantity to satisfy everyone's wants
10	Free goods	j	Best alternative forgone
11	Allocation of resources	k	An output combination to the right of the PPC
12	Entrepreneurs	l	Buyers of goods and services
13	Unattainable production point	m	A payment for the use of land
14	Consumers	n	People who bear the risks of a business and who organise the other factors of production
15	Rent	o	What land, labour, capital and enterprise are used to produce

Part 2 Missing words

One way to become familiar with key economic words and terms is to use them. This exercise is designed to test your understanding of some economic words and terms in context.

Complete the following sentences by filling in the missing word or words:

1 It is not possible to eliminate _____ as _____ grow faster than economic resources.

2 The economic problem means that people have to make _____.

3 Most land is _____ mobile, but geographically _____.

4 If gross investment exceeds depreciation there is _____ investment.

5 The payment labour receives is _____, whilst _____ is the payment entrepreneurs receive.

6 A country's labour force can be increased by _____ the retirement age and _____ the school leaving age.

7 Output is _____, whereas _____ is output per worker hour.

8 A key role of entrepreneurs is to bear _____ risks.

9 Another name for a production possibility curve is an _____ cost curve.

10 A production possibility curve shows the maximum output of _____ products with existing resources and _____.

Part 3 Calculations

Economists need to be able to write clearly, interpret data and undertake numerical calculations. At IGSCE/O level the calculations involve additions, subtractions, multiplications and working out averages and percentage changes. Your ability to undertake these calculations may be assessed on both the data response question on the Structured Question paper and on the Multiple Choice paper.

1 A firm employs 26 workers, paying each one $75 a week. What is the firm's total wage cost?

2 A country produces $900 million capital goods in a year. There is depreciation of $620 million. What is net investment?

Part 4 Interpreting diagrams

Economists make widespread use of diagrams. A diagram can be used to illustrate economic concepts, to analyse changes in economic conditions and to assess the effects of economic policies. Indeed a diagram can be worth a hundred words! Production possibility curves can be used to show a number of economic concepts including opportunity cost.

Figure 1.1: Different combinations of capital and consumer goods

Using Figure 1.1 state:

1 a The opportunity cost of increasing the output of consumer goods from 60m to 90m consumer goods.

b The opportunity cost of producing 80m capital goods.

Part 5 Drawing diagrams

It is important that you gain experience in drawing diagrams. Each diagram you draw should be clear and well labelled. You must use appropriate words on both the vertical and horizontal axes of a diagram. It is probably best to draw diagrams in pencil so that if you make a mistake, you can erase it and start again.

Draw a production possibility curve showing the effect of an increase in the quantity of resources.

Part 6 Multiple choice questions

Before answering a set of multiple choice questions, review your work on the topics covered. This preparation will build up both your understanding and confidence.

It is important to consider multiple choice questions calmly and logically. First read the question. You may want to highlight or underline key words. In some cases you may be able to think through an answer before you look at the options. For example, in question 2 below, you should consider what you understand by 'human capital'. Having decided on this, you should then look at the four options and select the one that comes closest to your understanding. This approach can also be applied to questions 7 to 10.

The other questions in this section are examples of those which you have to, right from the start, consider along with the options. For example, question 3 is an integrated question. You cannot provide an answer until you have read all the options.

In the case of both types of questions, you need to consider the options carefully. With some questions an option may stand out to you as correct. With other questions, you may have to arrive at the answer by eliminating the incorrect options.

Trust your judgement. Once you have selected an answer, move on. If you are finding a question particularly challenging, leave it and then return to it at the end. Never leave a question unanswered. If you have no idea of the answer, still attempt the question. You have a 25% chance of getting the answer correct.

When you have completed the multiple choice questions in a section, if you have time check over your answers and the explanations. It is particularly important to review the answers to any questions that you are unsure about.

1 What would cause an increase in the problem of scarcity?

A A reduction in resources

B A reduction in wants

C A rise in productivity

D A rise in the mobility of resources

2 What is meant by investment in human capital?

    A Encouraging immigration of people of working age

    B Paying bonuses to workers to encourage them to increase their output

    C Spending money and time on educating and training workers

    D Upgrading the machines labour works with

3 Which item is a factor of production?

    A The food a farmer produces

    B The satisfaction a farmer gains from his work

    C The tractor a farmer drives

    D The wages a farmer pays his workers

4 Which form of air is an economic good?

    A Air at ground level

    B Air from an air conditioning system

    C Air above an ocean

    D Air in a tropical rainforest

5 Which item used in the production of textiles by a firm would an economist classify as land?

    A Sewing machines

    B The factory

    C Untrained workers

    D Water taken from a river

6 What might be the opportunity cost of using a bus to transport students to school?

    A Increasing the earnings of the bus company

    B Paying the wages to the driver

    C Paying for the cost of petrol used

    D Transporting a group of retired people on a day out

7 What is meant by 'labour' in economics?

    A Hard physical work used to produce manufactured goods

    B Human mental and physical effort used in producing goods and services

    C Natural resources used in the productive process

    D Risk taking and organising the factors of production

8 What does a production possibility curve show?

    A The maximum combination of two types of products that can be produced with given resources

    B The prices of two types of products being produced

    C The quantity of capital and consumer goods that people would like to be produced

    D The relative profitability of capital and consumer goods

9 Which combination of economic concepts is illustrated by a production possibility curve?

    A Cost and price

    B Demand and price

    C Economic goods and free goods

    D Opportunity cost and scarcity

10 What does a point outside a production possibility curve represent?

    A A currently unattainable position

    B An inefficient position

    C The maximum use of resources

    D Unused resources

11 Four firms can produce soap and perfume. The table below shows the maximum number of bars of soap, and bottles of perfume, that each firm can make each day if they specialise in one type of product.

	Bars of soap	Bottles of perfume
Firm W	50	10
Firm X	60	12
Firm Y	64	16
Firm Z	90	20

Which firm has the lowest opportunity cost in producing perfume?

    A Firm W

    B Firm X

    C Firm Y

    D Firm Z

12 Which type of factor of production are a football stadium and an owner of a football club?

	Football stadium	Owner of a football club
A	capital	entrepreneur
B	capital	labour
C	land	entrepreneur
D	land	labour

Part 7 Similarities and differences

This activity will help you build up your understanding of aspects of the topics covered in this section.

Similarities

Identify **one** way in which each of the following pairs is similar:

1 Builders and teachers.

2 The entrepreneur and labour.

3 Forests and streams.

4 Wind and sunlight.

5 Production possibility curves and production possibility frontiers.

6 A production point inside a production possibility curve and a production point on the production possibility curve.

7 Finite resources and limited resources.

8 Forests and rivers.

9 Wages and profit.

10 A movement along and a shift in a production possibility curve.

Differences

Identify **one** way in which each of the following pairs is different:

1 Capital goods and consumer goods.

2 Economic goods and free goods.

3 Capital and land.

4 Geographical immobility and occupational immobility.

5 Opportunity cost and financial cost.

6 An increase in the quantity of an economy's factors of production and an increase in the quality of an economy's factors of production.

7 Consumers and producers.

8 Sunshine and a solar panel.

9 A production point on a production possibility curve and a production point to the right of a production possibility curve.

10 Capital and labour.

Part 8 Data response questions

The use of data puts economics in a real world context. In answering data-based questions, you should first read through the questions so that you know what you are looking for. Then read through the data. You may wish to highlight or underline key words. Having read through the data, return to the questions. Again you may find it useful to highlight or underline key words in the questions. For example, in the case of question 1c below, you may wish to highlight the words 'opportunity cost'.

To answer the questions, you will need to draw both on the information in the extract, and on your knowledge and understanding of economics.

In deciding how much time to devote to each answer, take into account the number of marks allocated. You should spend twice as long on a question with 4 marks than one with 2 marks. The degree of difficulty of the questions tends to build as the questions progress.

Study the source material for each question carefully and then answer Questions 1 and 2.

Source material: A new Indian car

On 11th January 2008, Tata Motors, part of India's Tata group, launched a new model, the Nano. On this day it became the cheapest car available, selling for half the price of the next cheapest car. For the price of $1000 a brand new Nano could be bought or, for example, a second-hand 1993 Land Rover.

The Nano is now produced in Sanand in Gujarat, in a factory which has the capacity to produce 250 000 cars a year. Tata Motors employs 2200 workers, including car designers, to make the Nano at the factory. With cars becoming more sophisticated, and the manufacturing process becoming more complex, the production process at the Sanand factory, and other car factories in India, is becoming more automated. Robots are now undertaking a number of functions that before were undertaken by humans.

The car was intended initially for the home market. It was hoped that millions could be sold in India. The firm also planned to export the car to Latin America, South-East Asia and Africa.

Although selling the car at such a low price made car ownership more affordable for more people, there were still many millions of people who would like a car, but did not have the income to buy one.

The sales of the Nano have not yet met the hoped-for level. In 2014, only 19 000 Nanos were sold. A year later sales rose, but only to 24 200. The cost of producing the Nano was higher in 2016 than its selling price which was then $1500. The disappointing sales and loss being made, led some people to suggest that Tata Motors should devote fewer of its resources to Nano cars and more to other cars. Others point out that Tata Motors could produce more types of other cars and save costs by closing a number of its factories, as most are working with spare capacity.

1 Referring to the source material in your responses, answer all parts of Question 1.

   a Identify an example of the factor of production labour used in producing the Nano. **[1]**

> **TIP**
> This is a straightforward question. You just have to select the relevant example and in this case, there is only one example. Do not waste time explaining why the example you have picked is an example of labour. The question only requires identification and not an explanation.

   b Calculate the average number of Nano cars produced per worker in 2015. **[2]**

> **TIP**
> For this question you would be credited full marks by just giving the correct answer. It is, however, useful to show your workings. This is because 1 mark may be gained even if a careless mistake has been made, if the right calculation has been undertaken.

   c Explain what was a possible opportunity cost of buying a new Nano car in 2008. **[2]**

> **TIP**
> The reference to 2008 should help you identify the relevant paragraph in the extract. As the command word is 'explain', it is not sufficient just to state what was the opportunity cost. You need to bring out the meaning of opportunity cost in your explanation.

d Explain **two** examples of the economic problem. **[4]**

TIP

Always pay attention to the number of examples, causes, reasons etc. that you have to explain. To avoid you writing about too many, or too few, the number of examples (causes, reasons and so on) is given in bold. Think first about what the economic problem is, and then find and explain two examples.

e Analyse **one** reason why the number of car workers may have recently declined in India. **[4]**

TIP

Note that only one reason has to be analysed. Analysis involves making links between points. Make sure you use relevant economic terms in your answer.

f Analyse, using a production possibility curve, Tata's output of cars in 2015. **[5]**

TIP

Draw a clear and accurately labelled diagram. Take into account whether the source material suggests that Tata Motors is currently using all of its resources or not. Make sure the diagram clearly supports your analysis.

g Discuss whether a car is a capital or a consumer good. **[6]**

TIP

This is an evaluative question. In this case, you need to consider both why it could be a capital good and why it could be a consumer good. In doing this, you need to bring out the nature of a capital good and the nature of a consumer good. There are certain key words and phrases that indicate that you are considering both sides. These include 'however' and 'on the other hand'. Towards the end of your answer, remember to consider the key factors that determine whether a particular car is a capital or a consumer good.

h Discuss whether the quality of workers used in producing Tata cars is likely to increase in the future. **[6]**

TIP

Draw on both the source material and your knowledge, and understanding, of the factors that influence the quality of the labour force. Consider both why the quality of car workers producing Tata cars may decline and why it may increase. Be careful to avoid making the same point in reverse. For example, stating that the quality will decline if educational standards fall is not adding anything if you have just written that it will increase if educational standards rise. All you have done is to identify educational standards as an influencing factor. If you want to mention educational standards both falling and rising you would need to establish in both cases why this might occur.

Source material: A German travel company considers its future

Some families take more than one foreign holiday a year. Not all families, however, are able to go on holiday whether at home or abroad. Most of those who take holidays would like to have more holiday breaks.

A German travel company in 2017 decided to stop selling holidays in Italy and instead to offer holidays in a new destination. This is the Maldives, a group of coral islands in the Indian Ocean, famous for their long hours of sunshine and sandy beaches. Tourism is a fast growing industry. The average price of a holiday for a family of four for a week was $2162 in 2017. Most tourists fly to the capital island Male. Many then sail to one of the coral islands that make up the Maldives and stay in relatively luxurious hotels or villas.

Tourists visit the Maldives from a range of countries. Table 1.1 shows the percentage share of the top five countries from which tourists came to the Maldives in 2016 and the share of world population of those countries.

Table 1.1: The main sources of Maldives' tourists and those countries' share of world population in 2016

Country	Percentage of tourists to the Maldives	Percentage of world population
China	30.0	18.5
Germany	8.5	1.1
UK	7.5	0.9
Italy	5.4	0.8
India	4.2	17.9

The Maldivian economy is heavily dependent on tourism and fishing. More than a third of workers are employed in these two industries. There is a greater range of jobs in the tourism industry including, for example, hotel chef and tourist guide.

2   Referring to the source material in your responses, answer all parts of Question 2.

    a   Identify an example of a free good.   **[1]**

> **TIP**
> Remember that for this question, your answer only needs to be brief – one word in this case is sufficient.

    b   Calculate the average daily price of a family holiday in the Maldives in 2017.   **[2]**

> **TIP**
> Calculations may come out as whole numbers. If they do not and you are not given further instructions, calculate to two decimal places.

    c   Explain what evidence there is of scarcity.   **[2]**

> **TIP**
> Provide the relevant example from the source material and explain why this is an example of scarcity.

d Explain, using examples, **two** factors of production involved in providing holidays in the Maldives. **[4]**

TIP
A straightforward question. Identify an example of two different types of factors of production from the source material and explain what type of factor each is.

e Analyse the relevance of opportunity cost for a travel firm in deciding how to use its resources. **[4]**

TIP
You can give a general answer here as well as drawing on the source material.

f Analyse, using Table 1.1, the relationship between population size and the number of visitors to the Maldives. **[5]**

TIP
First explain the expected relationship, then examine the extent to which the data supports this relationship and finally provide any possible explanation of any exceptions.

g Discuss whether hotels or hotel chefs are more mobile. **[6]**

TIP
Consider the two types of mobility.

h Discuss whether or not the Maldives will be able to increase its output of both tourism and fish in the future. **[6]**

TIP
The key here is to use production possibility curves.

Part 9 Four-part questions

This type of question has a stem which introduces and links the question parts. Each structured question is divided into four different parts. Part (a) is worth 2 marks and is a question which can be answered briefly. Part (b) carries 4 marks and involves straightforward analysis. Part (c) is worth 6 marks and requires more in-depth analysis. The last part, part (d), carries the most marks, 8, and involves the highest order skill, evaluation.

When selecting a structured question to answer, it is important to ensure that you can answer *all* of the question parts. It is best to answer the question parts in order as they may build on each other.

1   The economic problem will never be solved. This does not, however, mean that it will not be possible for some economies to produce more goods and services. It does mean that workers have to consider carefully what job they do and to recognise the benefit of being occupationally mobile.

    a   Define *the economic problem*.   **[2]**

> **TIP**
> A straightforward definition question.

    b   Explain the relevance of opportunity cost to a worker deciding whether to accept a new job and its relevance to the production of economic goods.   **[4]**

> **TIP**
> You will find it helpful to give examples here. The question does not specifically ask for examples, but they will enable you to clarify the points you make.

    c   Analyse the causes of an increase in the occupational mobility of labour.   **[6]**

> **TIP**
> It may be useful to highlight the word *occupational* so that you do not, mistakenly, analyse the causes of an increase in the geographical mobility of labour. Also note that the question asks you to analyse the *causes*. This means that you must analyse at least two causes.

    d   Discuss whether or not an economy could increase its output of consumer goods.   **[8]**

> **TIP**
> Your answer to data response question 2(h) should help you here, but be careful to pick up on the significance of consumer goods.

2   Pakistan is a major producer of cotton garments, knitwear and rice. To increase its output of a range of products, the Pakistani government is seeking to improve the quality and mobility of its economic resources.

    a   Define *an economic resource*.   **[2]**

> **TIP**
> A straightforward definition question.

b Explain what is meant by the geographical mobility of economic resources. **[4]**

TIP

This time, note you are being asked about *geographical* mobility.

c Analyse the reasons why a firm may increase the number of machines it uses to produce cotton garments. **[6]**

TIP

'Reasons' is plural, so analyse at least two reasons.

d Discuss whether or not there will be an increase in the supply of labour in Pakistan in the future. **[8]**

TIP

You do not need to have knowledge of what is happening to the size of Pakistan's labour force. You just need to apply your knowledge and understanding of the general influences on the supply of labour in any country to this question.

Answering four-part question 2

Below is a sample answer to question 2. The answer contains some common weaknesses. Read each part and consider how the answer could be improved.

a An economic resource is something that is used in economics.

b There are a number of causes of geographical mobility of economic resources. One is low cost of housing. The price of housing may be low where there are job vacancies.

c Firms may increase the number of machines they use to produce cotton as cotton can be made with machines. The machines may produce more cotton.

d Yes —
- Population may increase
- More women may enter the labour force

No —
- Workers may emigrate
- More people may go to university

Improve the answer...

Here are some ways to improve the above answer. Did you think about these?

a The answer is far too vague. It does not make clear what is meant by an economic resource. You should aim for precision in definitions.

b This answer does not bring out the meaning of the geographical mobility of resources. It does mention one influence on the geographical mobility of labour, but does not make clear it is labour that is being referred to. The last sentence is confused. It is more likely that the price of housing will be higher where there are job vacancies. This is because the shortage of workers is likely to mean wages are high and so people may be willing and able to spend more on housing.

c This answer is too brief and, again, too vague. The first sentence is not explaining why a firm may **increase** the number of machines it uses – just why it might use machines. The second sentence is not making it clear whether the machines can produce more than before and/or more than other factors of production. In addition, it does not analyse why this might be the case.

d This is a list-like approach. It does identify relevant points and it is two-sided. The answer, however, is not establishing the points. For example, why might an increase in population result in an increase in the supply of labour in Pakistan in the future? You have to show that you not only know the key influences on the supply of labour, but that you can analyse and assess these.

TIP

It is best to avoid a list-like approach. Only take this approach if you are running out of time in an examination. However, with careful time management, you should have sufficient time to explore the question in enough depth.

Learning summary

Before completing the activities in this section, review your work on these topics:

- Microeconomics and macroeconomics
- The role of markets in allocating resources
- Demand
- Supply
- Price determination
- Causes of price changes
- Price elasticity of demand
- Price elasticity of supply
- Market economic system
- Market failure
- Mixed economic system

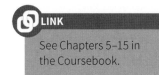

LINK

See Chapters 5–15 in the Coursebook.

Part 1 Definitions

In this section you have more terms to match with their definitions than you had in the first section. This may seem more challenging, but the practice you gained in matching terms and definitions in Section 1 should help. Some of the definitions may be expressed in slightly different words to those you are familiar with. However, if you understand the terms you should not have a problem.

Match the following terms with their appropriate definitions.

1	A market economy	**a**	A measure of the sensitivity of demand for a product to a change in its price
2	Extension in demand	**b**	This is where the quantity demanded of a product is equal to the quantity supplied
3	Increase in demand	**c**	A situation where market forces do not result in an efficient outcome
4	Supply	**d**	Products that are more harmful for consumers than they realise and which have external costs
5	A contraction in supply	**e**	Products which are both non-rival and non-excludable
6	Market supply	**f**	The willingness and ability to sell a product
7	Equilibrium price	**g**	The total benefits arising from producing or consuming a product
8	A subsidy	**h**	Spending by central and local government
9	A shortage	**i**	Products bought to be used together
10	Price elasticity of demand	**j**	A situation where demand exceeds supply
11	Elastic demand	**k**	A shift in the demand curve to the right

12 Complements	l	A movement along a demand curve as a result of a fall in the price of the product
13 Market failure	m	A movement along a supply curve as a result of a fall in the price of the product
14 External costs	n	The total supply of a product
15 Social benefits	o	A measure of the sensitivity of supply to a change in price
16 Demerit goods	p	A payment to encourage the production or consumption of a product
17 Public goods	q	An economic system which relies on the price mechanism to allocate resources
18 Government failure	r	Harmful effects on third parties
19 Public expenditure	s	When a change in price causes a greater percentage change in quantity demanded
20 Price elasticity of supply	t	When government intervention increases inefficiency

Part 2 Missing words

This activity includes twice as many sentences than in Section 1. Think carefully about the most appropriate word or words to complete the sentences.

Complete the following sentences by filling in the missing word or words.

1   Any type of economic system has to answer _____ key economic questions. One of these is how the products that are made are _____.

2   A mixed economy is one in which the allocation of _____ is determined by both the _____ mechanism and _____ intervention.

3   One of the advantages of a market economy is _____ sovereignty.

4   Economists define demand as the willingness and _____ to buy a product.

5   A _____ in the price of a product will cause a contraction in demand.

6   Rival products are known as _____, whilst products that are bought to be used together are known as _____.

7   A rise in the price of a product with inelastic demand results in a _____ in total revenue.

8   The more _____ defined a market is, the more _____ there are, so the more elastic demand is.

9   Price elasticity of supply is a measure of the responsiveness of _____ of a product to a change in its _____.

10 A market is said to be in _____ when demand is not equal to _____.

11 A market system can promote efficiency by putting _____ pressure on firms.

12 A decrease in demand for a product will cause a _____ in price and a _____ in supply.

13 There will be downward pressure on the price of a product if _____ exceeds _____.

14 A merit good has both higher _____ benefits than consumers realise and _____ effects on _____ parties.

15 Market forces will not encourage private sector firms to produce _____ goods as those wanting the products can act as _____ riders.

16 Social costs minus private costs equals _____ costs.

17 To encourage the consumption of a merit good, a government may provide a _____ to producers. In contrast, to discourage the consumption of a demerit good it may place a _____ on the product.

18 Information _____ can result in consumers paying _____ that are too high.

19 If a government overestimates the extent of external costs, it will set a tax that is too _____.

20 Taxation is one way of financing _____ expenditure.

Part 3 Calculations

Academic economists, and economists working for businesses and the government, frequently calculate price elasticity of demand (PED) and price elasticity of supply (PES) figures. Their findings can, for example, help firms to decide whether to alter their prices, whether they are responding fast enough to changes in market conditions and can indicate to a government which products to tax to raise revenue.

Answer the following questions, each of which starts with a calculation:

1 It is estimated that if the price of a bar of chocolate is changed by 4%, demand will alter by 6%.

   a Calculate the price elasticity of demand of this bar of chocolate.
   b Is the demand elastic or inelastic?
   c Explain one reason for the degree of elasticity you have found.
   d If the chocolate manufacturer wishes to raise revenue, should it lower or raise price?

2 A rise in the price of cigarettes from $6 to $9 is found to cause demand to contract from 200 000 to 140 000 a day in an island country.

   a Calculate the price elasticity of demand of cigarettes on the island.
   b Is the demand elastic or inelastic?
   c Explain one reason for the degree of elasticity you have found.
   d Would taxing cigarettes be more effective in reducing smoking or raising tax revenue? Explain your answer.

3 A rise in the price from $4 to $4.80 causes the supply of a bunch of freshly cut roses to extend from 500 to 525 a day and the supply of a bunch of artificial roses to extend from 200 to 280.

   a Calculate the price elasticity of supply of:
      i a bunch of freshly cut roses
      ii a bunch of artificial roses.
   b State, in each case, whether supply is elastic or inelastic.
   c Explain the difference in the degree of elasticity of the two products.

Part 4 Interpreting diagrams

A demand and supply diagram is the best known and probably the most frequently used diagram in economics. The economist credited with introducing this diagram is Alfred Marshall (1842–1924) who included examples in his famous textbook *Principles of Economics* published in 1890.

In this activity, study the demand and supply diagram, and then answer the questions which follow.

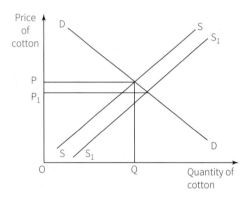

Figure 2.1: The market for cotton

a Complete the diagram.

b Identify what the change in the position of the supply curve is known as.

c Explain **one** possible cause of the change in the position of the supply curve.

Part 5 Drawing diagrams

In each case, use a demand and supply diagram to illustrate the effect on the market for a newspaper of:

a A rise in the price of a rival newspaper.

b A rise in the cost of print.

c A subsidy given to newspaper producers.

d More people finding news information from the internet.

e A major news story breaking.

Part 6 Multiple choice questions

In answering multiple choice questions on demand and supply, it is often useful to draw a diagram. For example, if a question asks what effect an increase in demand would have on price and supply a diagram, such as Figure 2.2, would help you to see that price would rise and supply would extend.

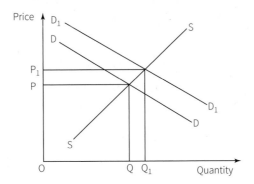

Figure 2.2: A demand and supply diagram

If you are allowed to use a calculator in your examination, become familiar with one that you are planning to use. Question 12 below may require a calculator.

1   Which feature is a characteristic of a market economy?

   A   Government planning plays a key role in the economy
   B   Producers respond automatically to changes in consumer demand
   C   Resources are allocated according to need
   D   There is always full employment

2   What is a mixed economy?

   A   One in which both capital and consumer goods are produced
   B   One in which both necessities and luxuries are produced
   C   One in which there is both an agricultural and a manufacturing sector
   D   One in which there is both a private and a public sector

3   A country changes from a planned to a market economy. What effect will this have?

   A   A decrease in government officials
   B   A decrease in the role of the price mechanism
   C   An increase in state ownership of resources
   D   An increase in the output of public goods

4   Which event would cause an increase in demand for petrol?

   A   An increase in concern for the environment
   B   An increase in the tax on diesel
   C   A decrease in disposable income
   D   A decrease in population size

5 What is meant by a contraction in demand?

    A A reduction in demand due to a rise in the price of the product

    B A reduction in demand due to a fall in the income of the population

    C A rise in demand due to a rise in the price of a substitute product

    D A rise in demand due to a fall in the price of a complement

6 Which event would cause the demand curve for air travel to shift to the left?

    A A fall in the safety of sea travel

    B A fall in the cost of air fuel

    C A rise in the price of foreign holidays

    D A rise in the size of the population

7 Which pair of products is an example of joint supply?

    A Beef and leather

    B Bread and butter

    C Cars and petrol

    D Computers and printers

8 Which change could explain the shift of the supply curve for a product from SS to S1S1 as shown in Figure 2.3?

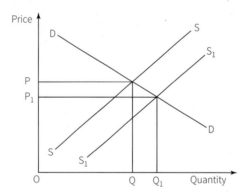

Figure 2.3

    A A fall in price from P1 to P

    B A rise in the quantity demanded from Q to Q1

    C A reduction in the cost of producing the product

    D The imposition of a tax on the product

9 What is meant by equilibrium price?

    A The lowest possible price for a product

    B The most profitable price for a product

    C The price which equates the demand for and supply of a product

    D The price which equates the number of buyers for and sellers of a product

10 Figure 2.4 shows the demand for and supply of gold mined in a country. Which combination of events could explain the rise in the price of gold?

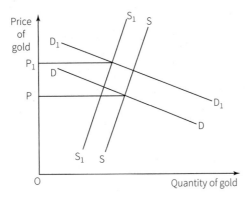

Figure 2.4

A A decrease in the price of silver and a subsidy given to gold miners

B A decrease in the taste for gold and an improvement in the technology used in gold mining

C An increase in incomes and an increase in the cost of mining gold

D A decrease in the taste for gold and an improvement in the technology used in gold mining

11 Why does travel by private jet have elastic demand?

A It is a luxury form of travel

B It is a necessity

C It has to be arranged some time in advance

D It has no close substitutes

12 A rise in the price of a product from $50 to $60 causes demand to fall from 800 to 760. What is the price elasticity of demand?

A −0.25

B −0.5

C −2.0

D −4.0

13 The price elasticity of demand for a product is −0.3. What effect will a fall in its price have?

A A decrease in total spending on the product

B A shift to the right of the demand curve

C A more than proportionate change in quantity demanded

D No change in the quantity demanded

14 What is meant by price elasticity of supply?

A The extent to which price changes when there is a change in supply

B The extent to which a firm can raise the price of a product whilst keeping the supply unchanged

C The responsiveness of supply to a change in the cost of production

D The responsiveness of supply to a change in price

15 Which advantage is a characteristic of a pure market economy?

    A   An even distribution of income

    B   Efficiency

    C   The encouragement of the consumption of merit goods

    D   The production of public goods

16 Which outcome is an example of market failure?

    A   Consumers paying a higher price for a product whose demand is rising

    B   Consumers exercising their market power by determining what is produced

    C   Producers basing their output decisions on private rather than social costs and benefits

    D   Producers earning a higher profit from switching from unpopular products falling in demand to producing those rising in demand

17 What would be evidence of abuse of market power?

    A   A failure to keep costs low

    B   A high level of competitive pressure

    C   A high level of mobility of resources

    D   A lack of profit

18 What is an example of a public good?

    A   Education

    B   Flood defences

    C   Healthcare

    D   Postal services

19 What is a reason for public expenditure?

    A   To increase external costs

    B   To provide support for vulnerable groups

    C   To reduce the mobility of resources

    D   To subsidise demerit goods

20 In which circumstance are private and external costs most likely to be considered?

    A   Assessing public sector investment projects

    B   Calculating a firm's profit position

    C   Deciding whether to use labour or capital to produce a product

    D   Estimating the effect of a change in price on the quantity demanded

21 A product's price elasticity of demand changes from -0.8 to -0.5. What does this mean?

    A   A rise in price will now cause demand to extend

    B   A rise in price will now cause total revenue to fall

    C   The product has become less responsive to a change in price

    D   The product has risen in price

22 What must it mean if social costs equal private costs?

    A External costs are zero

    B External benefits exceed external costs

    C Social benefits are zero

    D Social costs are equal to social benefits

23 Why are merit goods under-produced in a market economy?

    A These products are under-consumed

    B These products have an opportunity cost

    C It is not possible to make consumption of these products dependent on payment

    D It is not possible to produce these products at a profit

24 A product has a price elasticity of supply of 0.8 and a price of $60. By how much would price have to increase to cause supply to rise from 200 to 240?

    A $8

    B $15

    C $30

    D $48

25 A market is initially in disequilibrium. The price then falls to restore the market to equilibrium. What will happen to demand and supply as this movement occurs?

	Demand	Supply
A	contract	contract
B	contract	extend
C	extend	extend
D	extend	contract

Part 7 Similarities and differences

This activity will help you build up your understanding of aspects of the topics covered in this section.

Similarities

Identify **one** way in which each of the following pairs is similar:

1   What to produce and how to produce it.

2   A demand curve and a demand schedule.

3   Equilibrium price and a market clearing price.

4   Advertising and changes in disposable income.

5   Taxes and subsidies.

6   Perfectly inelastic demand and perfectly inelastic supply.

7 External costs and external benefits.

8 Information failure and abuse of market power.

9 Non-rivalry and non-excludability.

10 Market failure and government failure.

Differences

Identify **one** way in which each of the following pairs is different:

1 Individual demand and market demand.

2 Extension in supply and an increase in supply.

3 A market surplus and a market shortage.

4 Complements and substitutes.

5 Price elasticity of demand and price elasticity of supply.

6 Private expenditure and public expenditure.

7 Government failure and market failure

8 Merit goods and demerit goods.

9 External benefits and social benefits.

10 Conservation of resources and exploitation of resources.

Part 8 Data response questions

For activities where you are asked to respond to previously unseen data and information, you need to draw on both the data and your knowledge of economics. You will be expected to apply the economic concepts you have learned to interpret and analyse the data.

Study the source material for each question carefully and then complete Questions 1 to 6.

Source material: The world's growing taste for tea

The world price of tea fluctuated in 2016, but it rose at the start of 2017. Weather conditions had been favourable for the growth of tea. The main factor of production employed in tea production is labour and at the start of 2017 the productivity of the tea pickers in the main tea producing countries of China, India and Sri Lanka rose.

Although the supply of tea grew at the start of 2017, demand grew at a faster rate. For example, the demand for tea has been increasing in Pakistan for some time. Population and income has risen in the country. Tea drinking has also become more popular in Nigeria and Vietnam. In Nigeria, some people may have bought more tea because of the relatively large rise in the price of coffee in the country. In Romania demand for tea actually fell, although revenue from selling tea rose. This was because tea rose in price from $3.00 to $3.60 per kilogram and the price elasticity of demand for tea was −0.8.

Changes in the price of tea affect not only tea drinkers and tea producers, but also the demand and supply of other products. Figure 2.5 shows changes in the world consumption of tea and the world supply of milk between 2011 and 2016.

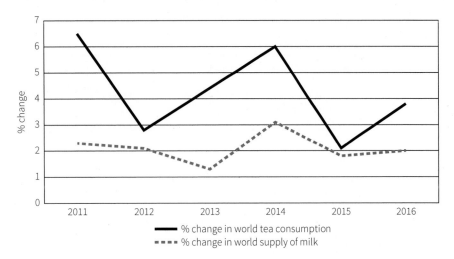

Figure 2.5: Percentage changes in the world consumption of tea and the world supply of milk, 2011–2016

The main tea producers are hoping that demand for tea will increase in the future.
They are, however, aware that there are risks involved in producing tea.

1   Referring to the source material in your responses, answer all parts of Question 1.

   a   Identify a determinant of supply.   **[1]**

   b   Calculate the percentage fall in demand for tea in Romania at the start of 2017.   **[2]**

TIP
You will find it helpful to be familiar with the PED formula here.

   c   Explain whether coffee is a complement to or a substitute for tea.   **[2]**

   d   Explain **two** influences on demand for tea other than changes in the price of related products.   **[4]**

   e   Analyse, using a demand and supply diagram, why the price of tea rose in 2017.   **[4]**

TIP
Label your diagram using the price and quantity of tea and make sure you explain what your diagram is showing.

   f   Analyse the relationship between changes in the consumption of tea and the supply of milk.   **[5]**

TIP
First consider what relationship you would expect to find between the consumption of tea and the supply of milk. Then examine whether the data supports this expected relationship.

g Discuss whether or not the demand for tea is likely to rise in the future. **[6]**

TIP

The source material and your answers to some of the previous questions should help you here, for example questions **c**, **d** and **f**.

h Discuss whether or not a country will benefit from producing tea. **[6]**

TIP

Again, the source material and your previous answers should help here.

Source material: Pollution builds up in Beijing

Beijing is one of the world's most polluted cities. Increasing industrial production and rising car travel is harming its air quality. It has been estimated that there are 1500 new cars on the roads of the capital every day. As well as creating air pollution, car travel causes noise pollution, congestion, injuries and deaths.

It has been estimated that the social cost of driving from Guangzhou to Beijing in 2017 was $450. Among the costs to the driver were the cost of fuel, the cost of tolls and maintenance. These costs, paid for by the driver, came to, on average, $220. In China owning a car is a status symbol and rising incomes are enabling more people to own and drive a car.

To try to discourage car travel in the city, Beijing officials have tried a number of policies. These include not allowing cars on the roads one day a week according to their number plates. It has been argued that the Chinese government should go further by reversing the recent increases in the price of public (mass) transport. One way it could do this is by subsidising bus travel. Some Chinese economists have also suggested that the government should upgrade the city's underground rail system so that it can operate more trains.

Beijing is not the only city suffering from air pollution. It has been estimated that air pollution kills more than three million people globally every year. This is more than the combined number of people who die from HIV, malaria and influenza. Table 2.1 shows the number of cars owned in six major world cities and the level of air pollution in those cities in 2016.

Table 2.1: Car ownership and air pollution in selected cities in 2016

City	Car ownership (millions)	Air pollution (concentration of particulates per cubic metre)
Delhi	8.0	153
Karachi	2.0	117
Beijing	6.0	56
Moscow	4.5	22
Los Angeles	6.5	20
London	2.6	14

2 Referring to the source material in your responses, answer all parts of Question 2.

   a Identify a private cost of driving a car. **[1]**

   b Calculate the external cost of car travel in Beijing. **[2]**

> **TIP**
> Show how you have calculated your figure. Show both the calculation and identify what concepts you have used to undertake this calculation.

   c Explain an external cost of driving a car in Beijing. **[2]**

   d Explain **two** reasons why demand for car travel has increased in Beijing. **[4]**

   e Analyse the relationship between car ownership and air pollution. **[4]**

   f Analyse, using a demand and supply diagram, the effect on the market for car travel of a subsidy given to producers of bus travel. **[5]**

> **TIP**
> Explain what will happen to the market for bus travel. You then need to analyse how this will affect the market for car travel. Your diagram should show car travel.

   g Discuss whether or not a reduction in pollution will benefit a country. **[6]**

   h Discuss whether or not Beijing officials should consider social costs and social benefits when deciding whether to upgrade its underground rail system. **[6]**

Source material: China: one country, two systems

Hong Kong returned to being a part of China in 1997. China has agreed that until 2047 Hong Kong can keep its own economic and political system, and have autonomy in everything except foreign affairs, defence and national security. The Chinese government decides the resources that are allocated to defence which are for good of the public.

Hong Kong's economic system comes closest to being a market economy, although it is not a pure market economic system. In contrast, China's economic system might be described as a planned economy moving towards a mixed economy.

Hong Kong is a high income and service-oriented economy, being particularly strong in financial services. Its market economic system has a global reputation for efficiency, with lower costs of production. Its consumers enjoy a wide choice of good quality products.

The area does, however, suffer from a number of aspects of market failure. For example, it suffers from a significant amount of air pollution which it is estimated causes 2000 premature deaths a year. Traffic congestion is also so severe that it is often quicker to walk than to drive on Hong Kong's major roads.

It is expected that over time, Hong Kong will develop an economic system closer to that of, for example, France. In France, both the private sector and the public sector play a key role in deciding what products are made, the methods of production used and who receives what is produced. Figure 2.6 shows a production possibility curve representing the French economy producing at point X in 2017.

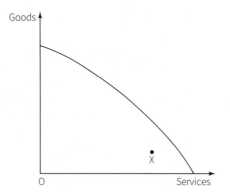

Figure 2.6: The French economy in 2017

3 Referring to the source material in your responses, answer all parts of Question 3.

    a Describe what type of economic system is operated in France. **[1]**

TIP

Questions may, but do not always, follow the order of the source material. In this case, the information that is useful to answer questions **a** and **b** can be found towards the end of the extract.

    b Identify, **two** of the fundamental economic questions. **[2]**

    c Explain, using information, **one** advantage of a market economy other than a wide choice of good quality products. **[2]**

    d Explain, using information, why no economy operates a pure market economic system. **[4]**

    e Analyse, the output of France in 2017. **[4]**

    f Analyse, using information, why traffic congestion can occur. **[5]**

TIP

This does not have to be a particularly long answer but you need to think through your answer carefully before you start writing it.

    g Discuss whether or not all consumers in a market economic system will benefit from a wide choice of good quality products. **[6]**

    h Discuss what type of economic system a country should operate. **[6]**

TIP

Try to be objective. Each economic system has its advantages and disadvantages.

Source material: Discouraging smoking in Australia

Smoking causes a range of health problems including lung cancer, heart disease, stroke, chronic bronchitis and emphysema. It also generates a number of external costs, including passive smoking and air pollution.

Demand for cigarettes is inelastic, although the degree of price elasticity of demand has changed slightly in recent years. This is because of the increased popularity of electronic cigarettes, first introduced in 2003, and the rise in the price of cigarettes. The supply of cigarettes is also inelastic, although less so than the demand. In 2016, it was estimated that the price elasticity of supply of cigarettes was 0.75.

The Australian government takes some of the harshest measures to discourage smoking. It bans smoking in public places, workplaces, restaurants and vehicles carrying children. Some local councils also ban smoking on beaches and sports grounds. Large fines are imposed on those who break the bans. The 2011 Tobacco Plain Packaging Act requires cigarettes to be sold in packets that are plain apart from health warnings. The government has also been increasing the tax on cigarettes. Between 2012 and 2016 the tax rose by 12.5%.

The increase in tax is the main cause of the rise in the price of cigarettes in recent years. Table 2.2 shows how the price of cigarettes and the demand for cigarettes have changed in recent years.

Table 2.2: The average price of a packet of 25 cigarettes and demand for cigarettes in Australia, 2012–2016

Year	Average price of a packet of 25 cigarettes in Australian dollars	Demand for cigarettes (millions)
2012	17.00	21 200
2013	18.75	21 350
2014	21.30	20 900
2015	23.65	19 242
2016	26.18	18 656

Smoking is declining in Australia. In 1977, 37% of the adult population smoked. By 2016, despite a rise in incomes, the percentage of the population who smoked had fallen to 13%. A higher proportion of the poor smoke than the rich. This is thought to be linked, in part, to the greater stress experienced by the poor.

4   Referring to the source material in your responses, answer all parts of Question 4.

    a   Does the Australian government believe cigarettes are over or under-produced?   **[1]**

    b   Explain what evidence there is that cigarettes are an inferior good.   **[2]**

TIP
Bring out the meaning of an inferior good in your answer.

    c   Calculate the percentage change in quantity supplied that would occur if the price of cigarettes rose by 20%.   **[2]**

    d   Explain **two** reasons why the demand for cigarettes has become less inelastic in recent years.   **[4]**

e Analyse the relationship between changes in the price of cigarettes and the demand for cigarettes. **[4]**

TIP
Think about the expected direction and extent of the relationship.

f Using a demand and supply diagram, analyse the effect of a ban on smoking in public places and workplaces on the market for cigarettes. **[5]**

g Discuss what information you would need to assess what will happen to the market for cigarettes in a country in the future. **[6]**

TIP
Assess what you think are the key influences on the market for cigarettes.

h Discuss whether or not a government should increase the tax on cigarettes. **[6]**

TIP
The key challenge here is to consider some arguments against raising the tax. The extract can help you with one.

Source material: Countries face world criticism for hunting whales

Japan, Iceland and Norway are seeking to end the ban on whaling for commercial purposes. They argue that government intervention is not needed and that market forces will ensure the right quantity of whales will be caught. Since 1982 the International Whaling Commission (IWC) has banned whaling for meat. It has, however, allowed whaling for purposes of scientific research.

Japan, Iceland and Norway have continued to capture and kill whales despite strong criticism from environmentalists, some economists and some governments. The Japanese government argues that whaling is important in order to find out the size of whale populations, their breeding and feeding habits. Others suspect that the Japanese whalers are mainly motivated by the profit that can be earned from selling whale meat to restaurants and supermarkets.

The IWC's scientists have calculated what they regard to be a sustainable catch of the most common whale species. But critics point out that there is considerable uncertainty as to how many whales there are. They also argue that it will be difficult to ensure that whalers keep to any limits set. Some governments with whales living off their coasts are also concerned about how whaling may affect their tourist trade.

Consumption of whale meat is decreasing. In 2015, it had fallen to an average of 30 grams per person in Japan. As incomes rise, people switch to eating other types of meat. In recent years, this tendency to switch to other types of meat has been encouraged by a fall in price of, for example, chicken. With higher average incomes, people also tend to eat more meat. Figure 2.7 shows the average income index and meat consumption in a number of countries in 2015.

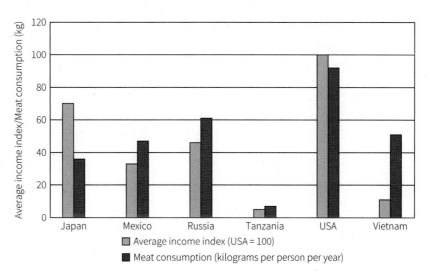

Figure 2.7: Average income index and meat consumption in selected countries, 2015

What people eat is influenced by a number of factors including not only income, but also regulations, subsidies and cultural differences in diet.

5   Referring to the source material in your responses, answer all parts of Question 5.

   a   Identify a government microeconomic policy measure other than a ban.   **[1]**

   b   Explain what type of resource whales are.   **[2]**

   c   Explain what is meant by a 'sustainable catch of whales'.   **[2]**

   d   Explain two causes of a decrease in demand for whale meat.   **[4]**

   e   Analyse the relationship between income and meat consumption.   **[4]**

   f   Analyse, using a demand and supply diagram, the likely effect on the market for whale meat of the removal of the ban on hunting whales.   **[5]**

TIP
Focus on what will happen to demand, price and supply.

   g   Discuss whether or not government intervention is needed to ensure an efficient allocation of resources.   **[6]**

TIP
You could use whaling as examples in your answer.

   h   Discuss the economic arguments for and against conserving whales.   **[6]**

TIP
This does not need to be a very long answer but you need to think through the points carefully before you start writing.

Source material: The price of basmati rice

The price of basmati rice fluctuates. In 2016, it fell due to an excess supply. The reduction in price resulted in a fall in revenue for the basmati rice farmers. In contrast in 2013, the price of basmati rice increased. There had been a poor harvest that year, whilst demand increased.

The aromatic, long-grain rice is grown in northern India and Pakistan, and is eaten throughout the world. People are, however, increasingly having a greater range of food items to choose from. For example, quinoa is becoming more popular because of the health benefits it is thought to possess.

The cultivation of basmati rice is relatively costly, and yields between one and two tonnes per hectare, compared with six tonnes for rival cereals. Wheat, for example, fluctuates less in price than basmati rice, and some basmati rice farmers are switching to higher-yielding and more profitable crops. Figure 2.8 shows how the world price of cereals and sugar changed over the period 2010–2016.

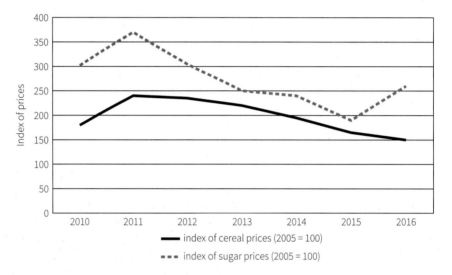

Figure 2.8: Index of world cereal prices and index of world sugar prices, 2010–2016

Attempts have been made to grow the Himalayan rice strain in Italy and some other rice growing countries. These have, however, failed to produce an acceptable product. Some basmati growers in India and Pakistan are trying to make the supply of the rice more elastic, but this may not prove to be easy.

6 Referring to the source material in your responses, answer all parts of Question 6.

    a Identify an opportunity cost to farmers of growing basmati rice. **[1]**

    b Explain whether or not demand for basmati rice was elastic or inelastic in 2016. **[2]**

    c Explain who is the entrepreneur in the case of basmati rice farming. **[2]**

    d Explain whether demand is likely to become more elastic or more inelastic in the future. **[4]**

    e Analyse the changes in the price of cereals and the price of sugar between 2010 and 2016. **[4]**

TIP

Be careful here. Figure 2.8 uses index figures. These show how prices have changed rather than actual prices. For example, while sugar has a higher figure at the start of 2010, it cannot be concluded that the price of sugar was higher than the price of cereals. What it means is that between 2005 and 2010 the price of sugar rose by more than the price of cereals.

f   Analyse, using a demand and supply diagram, why the price of basmati
    rice changed in 2013. [5]

g   Discuss whether or not it is easy, or not easy, to make the supply of a product
    more elastic. [6]

TIP

Make use of the influences on price elasticity of supply and remember the influence of time.

h   Discuss whether or not a government should subsidise the production of rice. [6]

Part 9 Four-part questions

**In answering questions on demand and supply, it is often useful to include diagrams
even when the questions do not directly ask for them. This is the case in question 1c.**

1   The number of cinema tickets purchased in the USA fell by 53 million between 2012 and 2016. A
    number of the states of the USA tax cinema tickets. India also imposes an entertainment tax on
    cinema tickets.

    a   Describe the relationship between demand and price. [2]

    b   Explain **two** of the main factors that influence the demand for cinema tickets. [4]

TIP

You could probably explain more than two factors. However, you do not need to explain more
than two. Indeed, explaining three or four is likely to mean that you will explain each in less
depth than if you had concentrated on the required two.

    c   Analyse how a government could increase the number of cinema tickets sold. [6]

TIP

Make sure you provide links between the measures you identified and an increase in the
number of cinema tickets sold.

    d   Discuss whether or not the government should impose a maximum
        price on cinema tickets. [8]

2   In 2016 the sales of smartphones increased most rapidly in the Philippines. The equilibrium
    price of smartphones has fallen in recent years. It is thought that demand for some
    smartphones is price inelastic.

    a   Define *equilibrium price*. [2]

    b   Explain, using a demand and supply diagram, why demand for smartphones
        has increased in many countries, but their price has fallen. [4]

    c   Analyse the factors that influence price elasticity of demand. [6]

TIP

A straightforward question that you should be able to write quite a lot about.

33

d Discuss whether or not price elasticity of demand figures are a useful source of information for a producer of a particular brand of smartphone. **[8]**

3 Poland is a former planned economy. It is now a mixed economy and is moving towards a market economy. A range of investment projects are being undertaken in the country including the building of a number of new airports.

a Define *a mixed economy*. **[2]**

b Explain why some countries are moving from a mixed to a market economy. **[4]**

c Analyse **three** causes of market failure. **[6]**

d Discuss whether or not a government or a private sector company should build a new airport. **[8]**

4 An increasing number of African countries are providing free school education. Mauritius has had free primary school education for some time and the government introduced free secondary education in 1977. The government also provides free healthcare and seeks to promote a more healthy lifestyle by taxing demerit goods.

a Define *a demerit good*. **[2]**

b Explain whether healthcare is a public good or a private good. **[4]**

c Analyse how resources are allocated in a market economy. **[6]**

d Discuss whether or not a government should provide free primary and secondary education. **[8]**

Answering four-part question 2

Below is a sample answer to question 2. The answer contains some common weaknesses. Read each part and consider how the answer could be improved.

a Equilibrium price is the price that consumers are prepared to pay.

b A rise in demand will shift the demand curve to the right. This will cause price to fall and supply to extend as shown in the diagram.

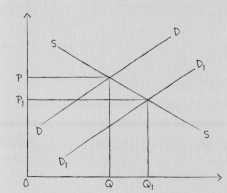

c There are a number of factors that influence the price elasticity of demand. One is price. The higher the price, the lower the demand. Income is an important influence. A rise in income will increase demand for most goods, that is normal goods. Demand for inferior goods would fall. Changes in the price of substitutes and complements are another influence. A rise in the price of a substitute will cause consumers to buy more of this product. A fall in the price of a complement would also increase demand for the product.

d PED figures are a useful source of information. If PED is greater than 1, it means that demand is elastic. In this case, a producer could raise revenue by lowering price. The producer should not raise price as demand will fall.

- If PED is less than 1, it means demand is inelastic. This time, a producer could increase revenue by raising price. It should not lower price as this will lower revenue.

- If PED is 1, it is unity, a change in price will have no effect. If the firm raises or lowers price, revenue will remain the same.

- PED figures are very useful to a producer as it lets him know what effect a change in price will have on revenue. Firms want to earn revenue as the more revenue they have compared to their costs, the more profit they will have.

Improve the answer...

Here are some ways to improve the above answer. Did you think about these?

a This is an incomplete answer. It is only considering the demand side and only part of the demand side as demand depends not just on what consumers are prepared to pay but also on what they are willing to pay.

b It would have been useful to have used a ruler in drawing the diagram and the axes should have been labelled. The most significant weakness here is that the student has drawn the demand and supply curves round the wrong way. The demand curve the student has drawn is actually the supply curve and the supply curve is the demand curve! This confusion leads the student into confused thinking as an increase in demand will cause price to rise. It is a rise in price which results in an extension in supply.

c The student has made a relatively common mistake, that is confused the factors that influence PED for a product with the factors that influence demand for a product.

d There are three weaknesses with this answer. One is that the points are not always fully established. For example, the student writes 'In this case, a producer could raise revenue by lowering price' but does not explain why. The candidate also writes 'The producer should not raise price as demand will fall.' This statement does not distinguish between elastic demand and perfectly inelastic demand as the inverse relationship occurs in both cases. Another weakness is that the student does not apply PED to a particular brand of smartphones as required by the question. The last weakness is that the answer does not evaluate as it only considers why PED figures may be a useful source of information and not why they might not be.

Learning summary

Before completing the activities in this section, review your work on these topics:

- Money and banking
- Households
- Workers
- Trade unions
- Firms
- Firms and production
- Firms' costs, revenue and objectives
- Market structure

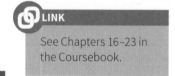

LINK

See Chapters 16–23 in the Coursebook.

Part 1 Definitions

This is a similar activity to previous sections. In some cases, such as *a* and *t*, *b* and *d*, *c* and *s* the definitions may appear at first glance to be similar. Closer examination, however, should reveal that they are not.

Match the following terms with their appropriate definitions.

1	Specialisation	**a**	The aim of making as much profit as possible
2	Division of labour	**b**	Organisations of workers that act in the interests of their members
3	Money	**c**	Disposable income that is not spent
4	Legal tender	**d**	Organisations of workers negotiating with representatives of employers
5	Tertiary sector	**e**	A lower limit set by the government on the pay of workers
6	Average cost	**f**	Wages plus other payments to workers
7	Profit maximisation	**g**	A payment based on the productivity of workers
8	Average variable cost	**h**	Total variable cost divided by output
9	Piece rate system	**i**	A form of money that has to be accepted in settlement of a debt
10	Trade unions	**j**	The stage of production involved with the production of services
11	Elasticity of supply of labour	**k**	Total cost divided by output
12	Earnings	**l**	Workers undertaking particular tasks
13	Wage differentials	**m**	An item used to buy products
14	Job security	**n**	Differences in wages earned by different groups of workers
15	National minimum wage	**o**	Earning as much revenue as possible
16	Collective bargaining	**p**	Protection from being made redundant
17	Savings	**q**	The extent to which the supply of labour alters when the wage rate changes

18	Savings ratio	r	The concentration on particular tasks or products
19	Sales revenue maximisation	s	The proportion of disposable income that is not spent
20	Profit	t	An excess of revenue over costs
21	Monopoly	u	Two firms that operate in different industries combining
22	Barriers to entry	v	Lower long run average costs resulting from the growth of a firm
23	Conglomerate merger	w	Higher long run average costs resulting from the industry growing too large
24	Rationalisation	x	A market situation with only one seller
25	External diseconomies of scale	y	Reorganisation of production to reduce costs
26	Internal economies of scale	z	Circumstances that make it difficult or impossible for new firms to enter a market

Part 2 Missing words

Some of the sentences here require you to fill in a number of words and four have only one missing word. Think carefully about the most appropriate words. You may find it useful to read out the sentence aloud once you have put in the words to make sure it makes sense.

Complete the following sentences by filling in the missing word or words.

1   Workers _____ can be referred to as _____ of labour.

2   Two of the functions of money are to act as a _____ of exchange and a _____ for _____ payments.

3   The key characteristic that an item has to possess to act as _____ is that it is _____ _____.

4   A _____ bank acts as the bank to the government and issues _____ and _____.

5   _____ is the price of _____ money and the reward for _____ .

6   Financial economies of scale involve a lower _____ and greater _____ of raising finance.

7   A group of workers is likely to be highly paid if demand for their labour is _____ and the supply of their labour is _____.

8   Earnings minus overtime pay equals the _____ paid to a worker.

9   A worker may be prepared to stay in a relatively low paid job if it has good fringe _____, _____ working hours and long _____.

10   _____ workers are usually better paid than unskilled workers because they are _____ productive.

11   A national minimum wage will raise the pay of _____ paid workers if it is set _____ the market _____ wage rate.

12   An increase in demand for pilots will be likely to _____ the wage rate of pilots and cause the supply of labour services of pilots to _____.

13   The supply of labour to a particular occupation refers to the number of _____ of work offered by the labour _____.

14 Elasticity of _____ of labour measures the responsiveness of the supply of labour to a change in the _____ rate.

15 A trade union is likely to have more bargaining _____ if unemployment is _____ and its workers are _____ skilled.

16 As people become richer, they usually spend more in total but a _____ proportion of their disposable _____.

17 People tend to save more if the rate of interest _____ and income tax is _____.

18 Dissaving occurs when people spend more than their _____.

19 The poor tend to have a higher average propensity to _____ and a lower average propensity to _____ than the rich.

20 Real disposable income is income that has been adjusted for _____ and after the deduction of _____ taxes.

21 Fishing is an example of a _____ sector industry whilst the production of toys is an example of a _____ sector industry.

22 State-owned enterprises are in the _____ sector.

23 If it is thought that a _____ corporation will work more efficiently in the _____ sector, a government may decide on _____.

24 As an economy develops, resources tend to move first from the _____ sector to the _____ sector and then to the _____ sector.

25 _____ costs are costs which do not alter in the _____ run even when the amount produced changes.

26 Average _____ cost minus average variable cost equals average _____ cost.

27 Total revenue divided by the quantity sold equals _____ revenue which is the same as _____.

28 A firm's _____ would increase if the gap between its _____ and costs increased.

29 A market in which there is a low degree of _____ concentration and free _____ and exit is described as highly _____.

30 A monopoly has _____ to entry and exit which can enable it to enjoy _____ profit.

31 A firm may remain _____ because of the _____ _____of its _____ or because the owner is experiencing difficulty raising _____ to expand.

32 A decrease in a long run _____ cost curve may be caused by _____ of scale.

33 As a firm grows in size, it may diversify. This would enable it to take advantage of _____ _____ economies.

34 If a firm reduces its output, its _____ cost may rise as it may no longer receive a _____ when it buys its raw materials.

35 Those running a firm may be more concerned with _____ rather than profit maximisation as their salaries and status may be more linked to the size of a firm.

36 A rise in output must reduce average _____ cost.

37 External growth of a firm may be the result of a _____ .

38 In the short run it is not possible to alter all the factors of _____ employed. The one which is usually in fixed _____ is capital.

39 Oil production is _____ intensive whilst catering is _____ intensive.

40 A monopolist is a price _____ and so as its output and sales rise its _____ revenue falls.

Part 3 Calculations

You will need a calculator to carry out these calculations. You may find it helpful to revise the definitions of costs before attempting them.

1 A small firm employs nine workers. The wages it pays to these workers are $200, $220, $280, $300, $310, $320, $330, $350 and $390 a week. What is the average wage paid?

2 A firm employs 85 workers and its total output is 2210 units. What is the average product of labour?

3 A firm's total cost increases from $400 to $700 when it produces its first unit of output. The output of a second unit raises total cost by a further $200. What is the average variable cost of the second unit?

4 A firm's average fixed cost is $10 and its average variable cost is $80. Its total cost is $3960. What is its output?

Part 4 Interpreting diagrams

Question 1 is based on applying demand and supply analysis to a labour market.

1 a Identify the equilibrium wage rate.

b Explain why the demand curve is downward sloping whilst the supply curve is upward sloping.

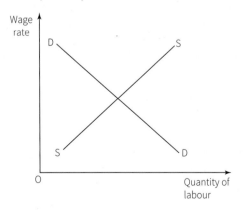

Figure 3.1: The market for labour

2 The diagram shows a firm's cost curves. Label them appropriately.

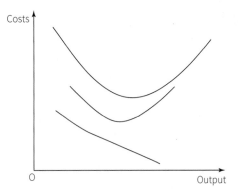

Figure 3.2: Cost curves

Part 5 Drawing diagrams

1 Using a demand and supply diagram in each case, show the effect on the wage rate of university law professors due to:

   a An increase in the number of students studying law

   b A decrease in the wage rate of lawyers

   c An increase in the qualifications needed to become a university professor of law.

2 In each case, draw a cost curve diagram to show:

   a Internal economies of scale

   b External economies of scale

   c Internal diseconomies of scale

   d External diseconomies of scale.

Part 6 Multiple choice questions

All questions in a multiple choice examination receive the same number of marks. Some questions, however, require more careful consideration than others. So do not worry if you find yourself spending more time on some questions than others. For example, you may find that you can arrive at a correct answer for question 19 more quickly than you can for question 11.

1 What does the extent to which workers can specialise depend on?

   A Division of labour

   B Opportunity cost

   C Taxation

   D The size of the market

2 Which function of money is most closely linked to saving?

    A Medium of exchange

    B Standard for deferred payment

    C Store of value

    D Unit of account

3 Why might division of labour increase unit costs?

    A Days lost due to sickness may be reduced

    B Labour turnover may be higher

    C Training time may be reduced

    D Workers may concentrate on what they are best at

4 What is the main form of money used in Europe?

    A Bank accounts

    B Coins

    C Gold

    D Notes

5 Which feature is a characteristic of money?

    A Durability

    B Indivisibility

    C Intrinsic value

    D Unlimited supply

41

6 What impact would an increase in the rate of interest be likely to have on borrowing and saving?

	Borrowing	**Saving**
A	decrease	decrease
B	decrease	increase
C	increase	increase
D	increase	decrease

7 Which change would lead to a rise in consumer expenditure?

    A A fall in optimism

    B A fall in saving

    C A rise in interest rates

    D A rise in income tax

8 What is a main function of a commercial bank?

    A To hold the country's reserves of foreign currency

    B To issue the shares of companies

    C To lend to its customers

    D To regulate the banking system

9 In which situation would the demand for labour be inelastic?

   A Demand for the product produced is elastic

   B It is difficult to replace workers with machines

   C It takes a short time to train new workers

   D There is high unemployment in the economy

10 Which one of the following types of trade union represents engineers?

   A Craft union

   B General Union

   C Industrial union

   D White collar union

11 A trade union persuades an employer to raise the wage he pays his workers above the equilibrium level. What is the most likely outcome?

   A More workers will be employed as it will be easier to recruit them

   B Some workers who retire or leave for other jobs will not be replaced

   C The firm will increase its output to raise the revenue needed to pay the higher wages

   D The firm will raise the wage rate higher to ensure demand equals supply

12 Which characteristic would strengthen the power of a trade union?

   A Demand for the product produced by the workers is elastic

   B It is difficult to substitute the workers by machines

   C Its members are unwilling to take industrial action

   D The wages form a high proportion of the industry's total cost

13 When is a labour market in equilibrium?

   A When the degree of elasticity of demand for labour equals the degree of elasticity of supply of labour

   B When the number of hours of work demanded is equal to the number of hours supplied

   C When the number of workers employed equals the number of machines in use

   D When the number of workers is equal to the number of employers

14 Figure 3.3 shows the market for bus drivers.

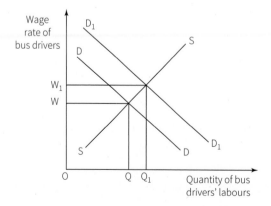

Figure 3.3: Again MC questions do not have diagram captions

What change could have caused the change in the wage rate paid to bus drivers?

A A decrease in the qualifications needed to be a bus driver

B A decrease in the wage paid to train drivers

C An improvement in the bus drivers' working conditions

D An increase in bus travel

15 What could cause an extension in the supply of farm workers' labour?

A A decrease in the number of hours farm workers have to work

B A decrease in the dangers included in farm work

C An increase in the wage rate paid to farm workers

D An increase in the non-wage benefits received by farm workers

16 Which change in the nature of a job would be most likely to increase the number of people willing to do it?

A A decrease in job satisfaction

B A decrease in holiday entitlement

C An increase in job insecurity

D An increase in on-the-job training

17 Which group of workers is likely to spend and save the most?

A Cleaners

B Doctors

C Factory workers

D Railway porters

18 A woman's disposable income is $300 and she spends $270. What is her average propensity to save?

A 0.1

B 0.3

C 0.7

D 0.9

19 Which group spends the highest proportion of their total expenditure on leisure goods and services?

A The poor

B The middle income group

C The rich

D The very rich

20 A trade union representing workers in a particular industry carries out a variety of activities. Which one of these may increase the profits of the firms in the industry?

A Operating a closed shop

B Promoting the training of workers

C Taking strike action

D Working to rule

21 What may be the opportunity cost to a worker of him specialising?

    A Concentrating on a particular interest

    B Concentrating on a particular job

    C Developing in-depth skills on particular tasks

    D Developing a range of skills

22 Student X leaves school early whilst Student Y continues into higher education. How are their spending and saving likely to differ over their lives?

    A Student X's spending and saving will be higher than Student Y's

    B Student Y's spending and saving will be higher than Student X's

    C Student X's spending will be higher than Student Y's but his saving will be lower

    D Student X's spending will be lower than Student Y's but his saving will be higher

23 Why might a worker leave a well paid job for a low paid job?

    A The low paid job offers fewer fringe benefits

    B The low paid job requires longer working hours

    C The well paid job offers better promotion chances

    D The well paid job provides shorter holidays

24 Which stage of production covers house building?

    A Primary

    B Secondary

    C Tertiary

    D Quaternary

25 A firm's fixed cost is $4000 a week. The average total cost of producing its output is $5 and its average variable cost is $3 a week. What is its weekly output?

    A 500

    B 800

    C 1000

    D 2000

26 The table below shows the total cost of a firm at different levels of output.

Output	Total cost ($)
0	20
1	30
2	38
3	42
4	50
5	60

What is the average fixed cost of producing five units of output?

    A $4

    B $12

    C $20

    D $60

27 Which cost is a variable cost?

    A   Interest payments on a bank loan

    B   Pensions paid to former employees

    C   Rent paid to a landlord

    D   Wages of workers paid on a piece rate basis

28 What is meant by fixed costs?

    A   Costs that do not alter a firm's profits

    B   Costs that only change with output in the long run

    C   Total cost of raw materials

    D   Total cost plus variable cost

29 What is a motive for privatising an industry?

    A   To ensure production decisions are based on social benefits and costs

    B   To increase state control

    C   To reduce competition

    D   To reduce productive inefficiency

30 A firm sells 30 units of output which cost $600 to produce and it makes a total profit of $150.

What is the firm's average revenue?

    A $5

    B $15

    C $20

    D $25

31 What is a characteristic of a monopoly?

    A   A low market concentration ratio

    B   High barriers to entry and exit

    C   Many buyers and sellers

    D   Perfect knowledge about market conditions

32 Why may a monopoly benefit consumers?

    A   It may restrict output to drive up prices

    B   It may restrict the entry of new firms into the industry

    C   It may spend some of its supernormal profits on research and development

    D   It may use some of its high revenue to pay large bonuses to directors

33 The directors of a firm decide to buy out another firm in the same industry. This is despite the fact that a report indicates that the new combined firm will experience diseconomies of scale. What is likely to be the short-term objective of the directors?

    A   Diversification

    B   Growth

    C   Profit maximisation

    D   Reduced market share

34 Which combination of circumstances is most likely to encourage a firm to invest?

	Rate of interest	Retained profits
A	high	high
B	high	low
C	low	low
D	low	high

35 What could explain a rise in a firm's production but a fall in the productivity of the labour it employs?

A Higher wages paid to workers

B Improved training

C Less skilled workers being recruited

D More efficient machines being used

36 Which type of merger aims to ensure control of retail outlets?

A Conglomerate

B Horizontal

C Vertical backwards

D Vertical forwards

37 A confectionery manufacturer buys a local newspaper. What type of merger is this?

A Conglomerate integration

B Horizontal integration

C Vertical integration backwards

D Vertical integration forwards

38 Which economy of scale is an external economy?

A Ability to buy raw materials in bulk

B Ancillary industries providing goods and services for the industry

C Costs reduction achieved by using more efficient machines

D More efficient use of the skills of workers

39 Which feature is an advantage of small scale production?

A Diversification

B Division of labour

C Economies of scale

D Flexible production

40 What can cause internal economies of scale?

A A firm's costs rising by more than its output

B A reduction in a firm's productive efficiency

C An increase in the size of a firm's factories

D A rise in the number of firms in the industry

41 What is likely to be a feature of an industry using capital-intensive production methods?

  A High concentration on personal services
  B High set-up costs
  C Low barriers to entry
  D Low proportion of capital employed

42 What is meant by profit satisficing?

  A Achieving as much profit as possible
  B Breaking even, with revenue equalling cost
  C Ensuring that the profit earned is more than rival firms
  D Forgoing some profit to achieve other goals

43 A firm has variable costs of $40 000 and fixed costs of $10 000. If its output is 500, what is the average cost and the average variable cost?

	Average cost	Average variable cost
A	$60	$20
B	$60	$80
C	$100	$80
D	$100	$20

Part 7 Similarities and differences

Two benefits of this activity are that it should help to clarify your understanding and help you to remember examples of various economic topics.

Similarities

Identify **one** way in which each of the following pairs is similar:

1 Specialisation and division of labour.

2 Unit of account and standard for deferred payments.

3 Bonus and overtime payment.

4 Working conditions and working hours.

5 Trade unions and professional organisations.

6 The Federal Reserve Bank of the USA and the Reserve Bank of India.

7 Overdrafts and bank loans.

8 Time rates and piece rates.

9 Location and career prospects.

10 Work to rule and overtime ban.

11 Survival and social welfare.

12 Choice and lower price.

13 Advances in technology and a cut in corporation tax.

14 Average fixed cost and average variable cost.

15 Overheads and fixed costs.

16 Sales revenue maximisation and profit maximisation.

17 A patent and brand loyalty.

18 Barriers to entry and barriers to exit.

19 Vertical integration backwards and vertical integration forwards.

20 Risk bearing economies and managerial economies.

Differences

This activity should help you to avoid confusing some key terms and appreciate to a greater extent some key differences. Identify **one** way in which each of the following pairs is different:

1 Specialisation and diversification.

2 Wage and non-wage factors.

3 Public sector and private sector.

4 External finance and internal finance.

5 Wages and earnings.

6 Equilibrium wage rate and disequilibrium wage rate.

7 A craft union and an industrial union.

8 Wealth and income.

9 Earned income and investment income.

10 Saving and dissaving.

11 A firm and an industry.

12 Profit maximisation and profit satisficing.

13 Fixed costs and variable costs.

14 Short run and long run.

15 Revenue and profit.

16 A competitive market and monopoly.

17 Normal profit and supernormal profit.

18 Internal growth of firms and external growth of firms.

19 Vertical integration and horizontal integration.

20 Internal economies of scale and external economies of scale.

Part 8 Data response questions

Questions which ask you to state or identify want a brief answer. It is important, however, that you write a full response when answering questions which require you to explain, analyse or discuss. Avoid using note format.

Study the source material carefully for each question, and then answer Questions 1 to 6.

Source material: Vast bonuses at commercial bank

Some banks pay their senior executives and star employees large salaries and give them large bonuses. Bankers are skilled workers. The average wage of bankers in Europe was $60 000 in 2016. The top earning employee of one Austrian bank received a payment of $5m in that year, consisting of her wage plus a bonus worth 25% of her wage. While the top earners in banks enjoy high wages and often receive spectacular bonuses they also work long hours, often under pressure. Some banks have made a number of their staff redundant in recent years, but generally bank employees experience a high level of job security.

Not everyone who works in a bank is highly rewarded for their work. The average wage of cleaners working for European banks was $9000 in 2016. Cleaners have less bargaining power than bankers. Despite this, in June 2016, cleaners at a US bank based in London went on strike over low pay and poor working conditions.

The profits of banks have varied quite considerably in recent years. Favourable market conditions when incomes are rising can enable banks to make large profits from lending. Recent financial crisis have, however, made some households and firms more reluctant to borrow.

Figure 3.4 shows how European banks' profits and bankers' wages have changed in recent years.

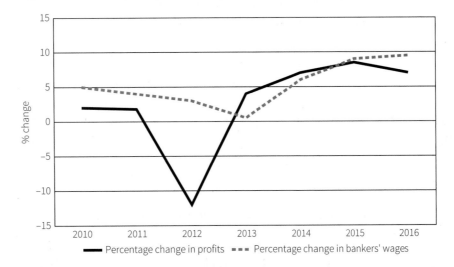

Figure 3.4: Percentage change in European banks' profits and bankers' wages, 2010–2016

1 Referring to the source material in your responses, answer all parts of Question 1.

a Identify **one** function of a bank.   [1]

b Calculate the bonus, in dollars, that the top employee in the Austrian bank received.   [2]

> **TIP**
> Take care with this calculation. It is not as straightforward as you might think.

c Explain a non-monetary advantage of working for a bank.   [2]

d Explain how favourable market conditions may result in a commercial bank enjoying record profits.   [4]

e Analyse the relationship between the profits earned by European banks and bankers' wages paid over the period shown.   [4]

f Analyse the reasons why bankers are paid more than cleaners.   [5]

g   Discuss whether or not high bonuses will prevent bankers moving from
    one bank to another bank.   [6]

h   Discuss whether or not cleaners would be likely to raise their wages by taking
    industrial action.   [6]

Source material: Should the government force people to save more?

The amount people save varies from country to country. In 2017, the average household in Laos saved only $110 of its disposable income. This contrasted with an average of $20 400 saved by households in Singapore, a country which had one of the highest savings ratios in 2017. In that year, households in China saved 39% of their disposable income, households in India 28% and households in Singapore 24%.

Nearly a quarter of adults in Laos have no saving, mainly because they cannot afford to do so. Of those adults who do save, the top reason they give for saving is to meet medical costs. Other reasons given are to meet unexpected expenses and to pay school fees.

As well as differences in income, the proportion of income that households save is affected by differences in the rate of interest, differences in optimism, differences in the tax incentives given and differences in state provision of retirement pensions, education and healthcare. Some economists and politicians argue that people should be compelled to save an amount that will give them an adequate income in retirement. It is thought that some people are too short-sighted to save enough while others are confident that the government will look after them when they are old.

There are, however, problems with compulsory saving. It is difficult to decide what would be an adequate retirement income. Some people are also too poor to save.

Forcing people to save may discourage some people from saving voluntarily. It may also mean that some people who are being made to save more than they want, may borrow to maintain their level of consumption. In both cases, national saving may not increase much.

The amount households save in Brazil has fluctuated in recent years. Consumer confidence has also altered in recent years. Table 3.1 shows how consumer confidence, based on surveys, has changed in Brazil and Singapore in recent years. Figure 3.5 shows the unemployment rates in the two countries over the same period.

Table 3.1: Consumer confidence in Brazil and Singapore, 2010–2017 (2010 = 100)

Year	Index of Consumer Confidence (2010 = 100) Brazil	Index of Consumer Confidence (2010 = 100) Singapore
2010	100	100
2011	120	105
2012	80	98
2013	85	97
2014	105	93
2015	90	96
2016	74	94
2017	65	92

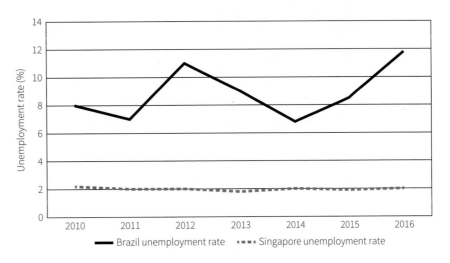

Figure 3.5: Unemployment rates in Brazil and Singapore, 2010–2016

2 Referring to the source material in your responses, answer all parts of Question 2.

   a Identify what is the opportunity cost of saving. **[1]**

   b Calculate the average household disposable income in Singapore in 2017. **[2]**

   c Explain what evidence there is of market failure. **[2]**

   d Explain **two** ways a government could encourage people to save more. **[4]**

TIP
The source material does not explicitly mention two ways but careful reading of the extract should enable you to identify two ways.

   e Analyse how unemployment can affect consumer confidence. **[4]**

TIP
Here you have to examine both a table and a graph. Given the question, it is logical to start with the graph.

   f Analyse why the level of saving may vary between countries. **[5]**

TIP
There is quite a lot of information you can draw on from the extract to help you answer this question.

   g Discuss whether or not the introduction of a generous state pension would reduce saving in a country. **[6]**

   h Discuss whether or not borrowing is likely to increase in Brazil. **[6]**

TIP

You do not need detailed information on Brazil. Your answer should be based on your knowledge and understanding of the influences on borrowing and the information given in the source material.

Source material: A boom in the Indian TV industry

India is experiencing both a rise in its population and a rise in income. Its industries are also being transformed by advances in technology. These changes are having an impact on the goods and services being bought and sold.

In 2017, 60% of India's 280 million Indian households had a TV. Ownership was greater in urban than rural areas but was increasing in both.

India is also forecast to become Asia's most lucrative pay-TV market with the number of households with TVs expected to double within a few years. Watching sport on TV is particularly popular in India. This high popularity has caused some people to specialise in producing TV sports programmes.

More TV channels are becoming available. In 1991, there were only two channels. By 2017 the number of channels had increased to over 800. One problem found in launching new channels is a lack of qualified production staff.

The growth in the TV market is having an impact on other industries in the country. A number of Indian cinema owners have expressed concern that the increased popularity of TV viewing would affect their revenue. As well as watching TV, people, particularly young people, are also using other forms of social media for social contact and for information and entertainment.

Figure 3.6 shows the relationship between the proportion of the population who have received secondary education and the proportion who use the internet.

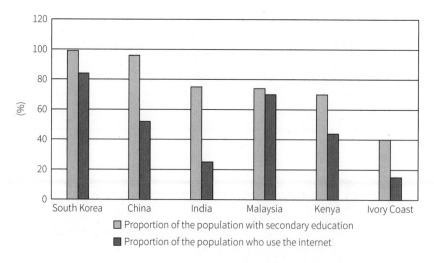

Figure 3.6: Education and internet use in selected countries in 2016

3 Referring to the source material in your responses, answer all parts of Question 3.

    a Identify one cause of an increase in demand for TVs in India in recent years.　　　**[1]**

TIP
Remember: you only have to state the cause, you do not have to explain it.

b Calculate how many million Indian households had a TV set in 2017. **[2]**

c Explain the likely relationship between TV viewing and cinema attendance. **[2]**

TIP
Use a relevant economic term here.

d Explain the evidence that suggests that the cost of running TV channels and making TV programmes in India is declining. **[4]**

e Analyse the relationship between the percentage of the population who have received a secondary education and the percentage of the population who use the internet. **[4]**

f Analyse, using a demand and supply diagram, what was likely to have happened to the pay of Indian TV production staff in 2017. **[5]**

g Discuss whether or not a person would benefit from specialising as a producer of a TV sports programme. **[6]**

h Discuss how easy it would be for a cinema operator to increase the sale of cinema tickets. **[6]**

Source material: German airports hit by workers' strike

At the start of 2017 there were strikes at four of Germany's main airports. Thousands of German ground crew staff, including baggage handlers and check-in staff, took the industrial action in support of their claim for a wage rise from 11 euros per hour to 12 euros per hour. The action was organised by Verdi, the largest public sector union in Germany. Verdi, which has large funds to support any industrial action it takes, asserted that workers in other industries had recently received similar pay rises.

The action taken led to hundreds of flights being cancelled and many passengers being stranded in German airports. The inconvenience caused reduced the public support the union had been receiving. Further negotiations between government officials and union leaders were expected. Not many people anticipated that these would be successful and union leaders were considering a range of further industrial action. The government was getting prepared to refer the case to independent arbitration.

A year before, the German national government and local governments, who own most of the shares in German airports, had reached an agreement on a previous dispute over pay which had resulted not only in strikes but also working to rule and other measures.

In 2016, there were strikes by other public sector workers affecting, for instance, hospitals and town halls. There were also strikes by private sector workers. The IG Metall metal workers' union organised strikes pressing for wage rises for the country's metal workers. Union leaders based their claims on the premise that higher wages were needed as it was becoming increasingly difficult for employers to recruit workers to the industry and because the productivity of their members had risen.

Despite these strikes, industrial action is less common in Germany than in most European countries, as shown in Table 3.2.

Table 3.2: Wage rises and industrial action in selected European countries, 2010–2015

Country	Percentage change in real wages, 2010–2015	Average days worked due to industrial action (per 1000 employees), 2010–2015
Cyprus	–9.4	490
France	11.0	170
Germany	14.2	13
Ireland	2.1	42
Spain	1.5	65

Within a country, strikes tend to be lower in firms which claim to have social welfare as an objective with the entrepreneurs of the firms pursuing an ethical approach.

4 Referring to the source material in your responses, answer all parts of Question 4.

   a Describe what is meant by 'public sector workers'. **[1]**

   b Explain what is meant by arbitration. **[2]**

   c Explain **one** form of industrial action, other than strikes, that a union could take. **[2]**

   d Explain **two** factors that would increase the chances of a strike being successful. **[4]**

TIP
Remember that the relevant information does not have to all be in one place.

   e Analyse the relationship between wage rises and industrial action. **[4]**

   f Analyse **three** arguments a union might make for a wage rise. **[5]**

   g Discuss whether or not introducing an ethical approach would reduce a firm's profits. **[6]**

   h Discuss whether or not it would be easy for a firm to attract more workers. **[6]**

TIP
You may want to examine each way a firm might try to attract more workers before considering the general influences. You may also wish to assess the likely success of each influence as you go along.

Source material: US airlines make record profits

In 2015 US airlines made a record profit of $26bn. The rise was largely due to a fall in the cost of fuel. Indeed, despite an increase in the number of journeys undertaken, US airlines spent 35% less on fuel. Labour costs did rise from $41bn to $45bn. The airlines' total cost, which also included the fees charged for take-off and landing slots at the airports the airlines use, came to $170bn. Most of the airlines' revenue, 80%, came from ticket sales. Other sources of revenue include baggage fees and reservation fees.

Nearly 85% of the profits earned by US airlines went to the four firms which dominate the US market: American Airlines, Delta Airlines, United Airlines and Southwest Airlines. These four airlines face different levels of competition on different routes. For example, there is little competition on the route from Los Angeles to Philadelphia and from San Francisco to Philadelphia. There is more competition on the Chicago to Atlanta and the Dallas to Houston routes.

In 2015 some airfares were reduced, particularly on those routes where the dominant four airlines face competition from low-cost airlines. Consumers are becoming increasingly price sensitive but airlines are reluctant to get into price wars. Table 3.3 shows how the price elasticity of demand for tickets on four routes varies.

Table 3.3: Estimates of the PED on four US internal flights, 2015

Route	PED for tickets on the flights
Chicago to Atlanta	–2.8
Dallas to Houston	–3.2
Los Angeles to Philadelphia	–1.3
San Francisco to Philadelphia: business class	–1.1
San Francisco to Philadelphia: economy class	–1.5

As well as price, demand for air travel is influenced by a range of factors. These include, for instance, changes in income and changes in the rate of interest. A rise in income increases demand for air travel. In contrast, a rise in the rate of interest would be expected to reduce spending including spending on air tickets.

Some economists suggest that US airlines should move into other markets, such as rail transport, to spread their risks and because they may find they have the expertise to do well in the markets.

A number, however, mentioned that airlines risked reducing their profits by expanding the size of their firms.

5 Referring to the source material in your responses, answer all parts of Question 5.

a Identify a variable cost of an airline. **[1]**

b Calculate the amount of revenue US airlines earned from ticket sales in 2015. **[2]**

> **TIP**
> There are two stages to this calculation.

c Explain what is meant by 'price sensitive consumers'. **[2]**

d Explain **two** benefits of diversification. **[4]**

e Analyse how a firm could finance the expansion of its business. **[4]**

f Analyse the significance of the PED figures. **[5]**

> **TIP**
> There is also information in the main body of the extract which you should find useful.

g Discuss whether or not the expansion of a firm will reduce its profits. **[6]**

h Discuss whether or not a rise in the rate of interest will reduce spending. **[6]**

Source material: The balance of the South Korean economy

South Korea has a large private sector. For instance, supermarkets in the country operate in the private sector. There are a number of supermarkets, including US and European supermarkets. These tend to avoid cutting prices as they are concerned a price war may break out with price cuts made by one supermarket being matched by the others. Instead they try to increase their market share by advertising, providing good delivery services, stocking a greater variety of products and using loyalty cards.

Between 2000 and 2010, the South Korean government privatised a number of state-owned enterprises which affected government revenue and the level of competition in a number of markets. In recent years, there has been a change in government policy. In 2013, the sale of a state-owned bank was stopped. The government was concerned that a private sector bank might not lend to small firms in difficulty, might charge borrowers a higher rate of interest than a state-owned bank and might pay over-generous bonuses to its staff.

This decision was supported by the government's bank, the Bank of Korea. Governments' decisions on privatisation affect the relative sizes of their countries' private and public sectors. Figure 3.7 shows the relative size of the two sectors in five countries.

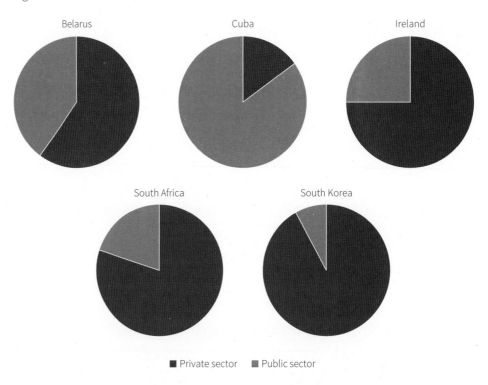

■ Private sector ■ Public sector

Figure 3.7: The role of the private and public sectors in five countries in 2016

6 Referring to the source material in your responses, answer all parts of Question 6.

   a Identify a function of a central bank. [1]

   b Explain whether or not banks operate in the primary, secondary or tertiary sector of the economy. [2]

   c Explain **one** reason why a firm may pay a bonus to its staff. [2]

   d Explain what effect the sale of state-owned enterprises may have on government revenue. [4]

   e Analyse how the role of the price mechanism would have varied in the countries. [4]

   f Analyse the ways a supermarket could use to attract customers apart from reducing price. [5]

   g Discuss whether or not the interest rate charged to borrowers by private sector banks would be lower than that charged by state-owned banks. [6]

   h Discuss whether or not consumers would benefit more from a competitive market or a monopoly. [6]

Part 9 Four-part questions

When selecting a structured question to answer, it is important to ensure that you can answer all the question parts. It is best to answer the question parts in order as they may build on each other.

1   The degree to which banks specialise varies, but all provide money transmission services.

    a Define *specialisation*.   **[2]**

    b Explain how money promotes specialisation.   **[4]**

    c Analyse the key functions of commercial banks.   **[6]**

    d Discuss whether or not a commercial bank should specialise or diversify in terms of the services it provides.   **[8]**

TIP

It is useful to answer structured questions in order. Such a strategy helps you to avoid overlap and assists you in putting together your answers. In this four-part question, writing about specialisation first, and then the functions of commercial banks, should clarify your thoughts on these topics and give you ideas on how to approach the part **d**.

2   India has a shortage of dentists. It is, however, expected that the supply of dentists will increase in the future. Changes in labour markets can have an effect on both the distribution of income and the amount people spend.

    a Identify **two** influences on the supply of labour to a particular occupation.   **[2]**

    b Explain why despite a rise in wages, people may spend less.   **[4]**

    c Analyse how a more even distribution of income may affect the pattern of expenditure in an economy.   **[6]**

    d Discuss whether or not dentists are always paid more than waiters and waitresses.   **[8]**

TIP

There are several economic concepts that can be applied on one side of the argument here. The challenge is to think of arguments on the other side.

3   In Bangladesh 48% of the labour force is employed in agriculture. Trade union membership has increased in the country in recent years. Most members of trade unions are public sector workers. The majority of farm workers are not unionised.

    a Define *a trade union*.   **[2]**

    b Explain **two** factors that influence demand for farm workers.   **[4]**

    c Analyse the reasons why some people may continue to be farm workers despite being offered better paid jobs as factory workers.   **[6]**

    d Discuss whether or not farm workers would benefit from joining a union.   **[8]**

4 The size of both the insurance industry and insurance firms is increasing in Argentina. Between 2012 and 2016 the country's largest insurance firm doubled in size, selling insurance worth $930 million in 2016.

    a Identify **two** ways a firm may become large. **[2]**

    b Explain what factors will influence the resources an insurance firm employs. **[4]**

    c Analyse the impact that the move into a larger rented office and the replacement of some of its temporary staff with permanent staff may have on an insurance firm's fixed and variable costs. **[6]**

    d Discuss whether or not the growth of the insurance industry will reduce an insurance firm's average total cost. **[8]**

> **TIP**
>
> You do not need detailed knowledge of the insurance market to answer this question although it is useful to remember that insurance is a service when you are answering **d**.

5 Car manufacturing firms are larger than car repair firms. Merging is a relatively common activity in the car manufacturing industry.

    a Explain the difference between total cost and average total cost. **[2]**

    b Explain why so many firms exist in the car repair industry. **[4]**

    c Analyse what type of internal economies of scale are available to a car manufacturer. **[6]**

    d Discuss whether or not a car manufacturer would benefit more from merging with another car manufacturer or with a firm selling cars. **[8]**

6 Tourism is a major industry in a number of countries. Merger activity is relatively high in the tourism industry of many countries. This is, in part, because it is thought that larger firms can cope better with fluctuations in tourist numbers. For instance, in 2015 the number of Chinese tourists visiting Kenya fell by 9%.

    a Define *a conglomerate merger*. **[2]**

    b Explain **two** possible reasons why the number of Chinese tourists to Kenya may decline. **[4]**

    c Analyse what impact the reduction in the number of tourists would be likely to have on the costs, revenue and profits of Kenyan hotels. **[6]**

    d Discuss whether or not a decline in the Kenyan tourism industry would result in unemployment in Kenya. **[8]**

Answering four-part question 2

Below is a sample answer to question 2. The answer contains some common weaknesses. Read each part and consider how the answer could be improved.

a The wage rate, the price of other factors of production, the demand for the product, working conditions, promotion chances.

b People may have more money but they may save more. Saving allows people to cope with unexpected expenses such as the cost of having their heating system repaired. Saving also provides funds for the education of their children. In addition, people save to buy expensive consumer durables such as washing machines.

c   A more even distribution of income can increase the amount that is spent in an economy. This is because the poor spend a higher proportion of their income than the rich. If income is redistributed from the rich to the poor, the poor will be able to buy more goods and services. The rich will have less income but they may not have spent all of the income they lose — they may have saved some of it. For example, $100 may be taken from a rich person and given to a poor person. The poor person may spend all of the extra income while the rich person may have only spent $40 of it. In this case, net spending will rise by $60.

d   Dentists are paid more than waiters and waitresses because they work harder. The job they do is more demanding and stressful. They are educated people and so they deserve higher wages. Waiting at tables is easy and so anyone can do it. This means that they do not have to be paid high wages.

But some dentists are not very good at their jobs and some do not have many patients. Other dentists may only work a few hours a week. In contrast, some waiters and waitresses may work long hours and may receive generous overtime payments. Indeed, waiters and waitresses often work unsociable hours.

Improve the answer...

Here are some ways to improve the above answer. Did you think about these?

a   The student here seems to be confused between the influences on the supply of and on the demand for labour in a particular occupation and appears to have written down every influence she could think of. The second and third influences identified relate to demand for labour. The question only asks for two influences, so it would be the first two which would be considered.

b   The answer here is rather narrow as it only considers one influence. It should also have been dynamic and not static. This means that it should have considered why spending may change (in this case fall) and not why it is at a certain rate. Despite the first sentence, the student concentrates on the reasons why people save and not why they may save more.

c   There is some good economics here. The problem is that the student is analysing how a more even distribution of income may affect the level rather than the pattern of expenditure.

d   The key, related, problems here are that the answer is based more on general knowledge and personal opinion than on economic theory and so it lacks depth. For example, 'they deserve higher wages' is a personal opinion. The application of demand and supply theory would have considerably strengthened the answer. For example, 'waiting at tables is easy and so anyone can do it' could have been linked to the training and qualifications needed and so to the supply of waiters and waitresses. The last two sentences are the strongest.

Government and the macroeconomy

Learning summary

Before completing the activities in this section, review your work on these topics:

- The role of government
- The macroeconomic aims of government
- Fiscal policy
- Monetary policy
- Supply-side policy
- Economic growth
- Employment and unemployment
- Inflation and deflation

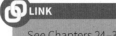

LINK

See Chapters 24–31 in the Coursebook.

Part 1 Definitions

Match the following terms with the appropriate definitions. Take care as some of the terms are very similar.

1	Full employment	**a**	The percentage of income paid in tax
2	The unemployment rate	**b**	A rise in the general price level caused by the money supply increasing faster than output
3	Economic growth	**c**	A policy that influences the price or quantity of money
4	Total demand	**d**	People out of work due to structural changes in the economy
5	Balance of payments	**e**	A very rapid and large rise in the general price level
6	Imports	**f**	A measure of the change in the price of a representative basket of goods and services
7	The consumer prices index	**g**	A situation where people are in between jobs
8	Monetary inflation	**h**	The demand for a country's output
9	Hyperinflation	**i**	A record of a country's economic transactions with other countries
10	Employment rate	**j**	A tax on companies' profits
11	The claimant count	**k**	A government's decisions on its spending and taxation
12	Fiscal policy	**l**	Products bought from other countries
13	Monetary policy	**m**	The proportion of people of working age who are in employment
14	Supply-side policy measures	**n**	Negative economic growth over two successive quarters
15	Proportional tax	**o**	A tax that takes an equal percentage of the income from the rich and the poor
16	Corporation tax	**p**	As low an unemployment rate as possible
17	Index-linking	**q**	Policies designed to increase an economy's productive capacity

18 Tax burden	r	A measure of unemployment based on those receiving unemployment benefits
19 Technological unemployment	s	An increase in real GDP
20 Gross Domestic Product	t	Those without work, but seeking it as a percentage of the labour force
21 Short run economic growth	u	Income payments not related to output
22 Frictional unemployment	v	An economy making fuller use of existing resources
23 The circular flow of income	w	Domestic output produced over a period of a year
24 A recession	x	The expense of changing prices as a result of inflation
25 Transfer payments	y	Adjusting payments to reflect changes in the cost of living
26 Menu costs	z	The movement of income and spending round an economy

Part 2 Missing words

You should now be very familiar with supplying the relevant missing words.

Complete the following sentences by filling in the missing word or words.

1   Price stability is usually taken to mean a _____ and stable rate of _____.

2   If _____ economic growth exceeds actual economic growth, an economy will be producing at a point inside its _____   _____ curve.

3   A government can redistribute income from the _____ to the _____ by raising progressive _____ and increasing the benefits paid to the poor.

4   A budget _____ occurs when government spending exceeds _____ revenue.

5   A deflationary _____ policy seeks to reduce _____ demand by raising _____ or reducing _____ _____.

6   Two of the qualities of a good _____ are that it is convenient to pay and that it is flexible.

7   _____   _____ are designed to raise revenue and discourage imports.

8   A government may raise its spending by too much if it underestimates the size of the _____.

9   Supply-side policies always seek to _____ aggregate supply and never to _____ it.

10   _____ taxes take not only more of the income of the rich, but also a higher _____ of their income.

11   A rise in the rate of interest is an example of deflationary _____ policy whilst a cut in income tax is an example of _____ _____ policy.

12   If a government introduces new taxes, but cuts tax rates, the tax _____ will widen whilst the tax _____ may fall.

13 Government measures taken to increase total spending may reduce unemployment, but may cause an increase in the country's _____ rate.

14 A shift to the _____ of a country's total demand curve and its total supply curve may raise both _____ and _____ economic growth.

15 To reduce spending on imports, a government may _____ income tax and _____ domestic producers.

16 Two of the stages in constructing a consumer prices index are selecting a _____ year and attaching _____ to different categories of expenditure.

17 Demand-pull _____ is likely to occur when an economy is producing close to full _____.

18 Inflation can redistribute income from lenders to _____ and from workers with _____ bargaining power to workers with _____ bargaining power.

19 Two ways of measuring unemployment are to count those receiving unemployment related _____ and to conduct _____ _____ surveys.

20 An increase in total (aggregate) demand should reduce _____ unemployment, but may not reduce _____ or _____ unemployment.

21 The effects of unemployment will be more serious, the _____ the unemployment rate and the _____ the duration of the unemployment.

22 An increase in unemployment may result in a budget _____ as tax revenue is likely to _____ whilst government spending on _____ _____ is likely to rise.

23 Real GDP is GDP at _____ prices and has been adjusted for _____.

24 For economic growth to continue it is important that both total (aggregate) demand and total (aggregate) supply _____ and that the growth is _____.

25 _____ _____ inflation is more likely to encourage producers to expand than _____ _____ inflation.

26 Public sector workers are employed by the _____ and may have higher job security than those employed in the _____ sector.

27 When people have been unemployed for a _____ time, employers tend to become reluctant to employ them and some become out of date with advances in _____ and working _____.

28 In the short run, economic growth may _____ the output of consumer goods, but it is likely to _____ their output in the long run.

29 Forms of government spending and taxation that alter without any change in government policy are known as _____ _____.

30 A reduction in inflation will reduce _____ _____ costs as households and firms will be able to leave money in existing bank accounts.

Part 3 Calculations

In some of these questions, the answer is a whole number or a number that goes to one decimal place. In questions where this is not the case, it is advisable to give an answer to two decimal places.

1　**a**　A country has a population of 20 million, a labour force of 12.5 million and 2 million unemployed workers. What is the unemployment rate?

　　b　In a country 3 million people are unemployed and 21 million people are employed. What is the country's unemployment rate?

2　**a**　A country with a total income of $20 billion has a tax burden of 40%. How much tax revenue does its government receive?

　　b　A person earns $30 000 a year, of which $25 000 is taxable. The rate of income tax is 20% on the first $5000 of taxable income and 30% on all taxable income above that level. How much tax will be deducted from this person?

3　**a**　The consumer prices index in a country rises from 150 to 153 over a period of a year. What is the rate of inflation?

　　b　Table 4.1 shows the weights and the price changes of three categories of products used to construct a weighted price index. Calculate the change in the price level.

Table 4.1

Item	Weight	Price change (%)
Food	½	5
Clothing	¼	10
Leisure goods	¼	16

Part 4 Interpreting diagrams

1

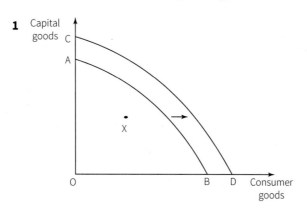

Figure 4.1: Changes in the macroeconomy

　　a　Describe what economic problem is illustrated by point X.

　　b　Explain what macroeconomic aim may be achieved by the movement from AB to CD of the production possibility curve.

2 An aggregate demand and aggregate supply diagram is a useful tool to analyse changes in the macroeconomy.

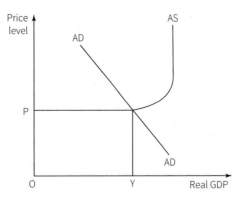

Figure 4.2: An aggregate demand and aggregate supply diagram

a Explain **three** of the labels in the diagram.

b Identify **two** possible causes of shifts in the AD curve.

c Describe what effect would an increase in AD be likely to have on inflation and employment in this case.

Part 5 Drawing diagrams

1 Use a demand and supply diagram to:

a Illustrate the effect of the imposition of an indirect tax on a product with perfectly inelastic demand.

b Analyse how the burden of the tax will be shared out.

2 **a** Illustrate the effect of the granting of a subsidy to producers of a product with elastic supply.

b Analyse how the benefit of the subsidy will be shared out.

TIP

In questions 1 and 2, the diagram you draw in part **a** should help you with the analysis in part **b**. Remember to explain who will be mainly affected by the tax and subsidy and say why.

3 In each case use a production possibility curve to illustrate:

a An increase in unemployment

b Actual economic growth

c Potential economic growth.

Part 6 Multiple choice questions

A number of the multiple choice questions in this section test your ability to distinguish between different types of macroeconomic policies. It is important to be able to differentiate between fiscal, monetary and supply-side policies. Remember: fiscal and monetary policies are designed to influence total demand whilst supply-side policies aim to increase total supply. There are a number of questions on taxation. Some questions on taxation incorporate both macroeconomic and microeconomic concepts.

1 The production of which type of products has to be financed by taxation?

    A Those that are unprofitable

    B Those that are both non-rival and non-excludable

    C Those that have higher social costs than private costs

    D Those that are luxury items

2 What is a macroeconomic policy objective?

    A To increase employment

    B To increase the output of the car industry

    C To reduce the price level

    D To reduce economic growth

3 Which change is most likely to reduce total demand?

    A An increase in investment

    B An increase in savings

    C A reduction in government tax revenue

    D A reduction in imports

4 What effect will a subsidy given to producers of a product have on the price and demand for that product?

	Price	Demand
A	decrease	contract
B	decrease	extend
C	increase	extend
D	increase	contract

5 How may fiscal policy increase total (aggregate) demand?

    A By cutting the rate of interest

    B By cutting the rate of taxation

    C By increasing the budget surplus

    D By increasing the money supply

6 Which policy measure is an example of monetary policy designed to reduce total (aggregate) demand?

    A A limit placed on bank lending

    B A reduction in interest rates

    C A rise in income tax

    D A switch in government spending from consumer to capital goods

7 What does a government's budget position show?

A How the exchange rate influences the country's trade position

B How the rate of interest influences the money supply

C The relationship between export revenue and import expenditure

D The relationship between government spending and tax revenue

8 What effect is a supply-side policy measure designed to have on a country's total (aggregate) supply curve and production possibility curve (PPC)?

	Total (AS) curve	PPC
A	decrease	decrease
B	decrease	increase
C	increase	increase
D	increase	decrease

9 Which policy measure would be classified as a fiscal policy instrument?

A A cut in the rate of interest

B An increase in the money supply

C The imposition of a quota

D A rise in government spending on defence

10 Which economic problem may cause a government to cut taxation?

A A current account deficit

B Cyclical unemployment

C Demand-pull inflation

D A high, unsustainable rate of economic growth

11 Which government policy measure may be classified as either a fiscal policy measure or a supply-side policy measure?

A A decrease in the exchange rate

B A decrease in the rate of interest

C An increase in corporation tax

D An increase in government spending on education

12 In which circumstance must a government be saving?

A When it operates a budget surplus

B When it privatises public corporations

C When it reduces government spending and taxation by an equal amount

D When it switches from relying on direct taxes to relying on indirect taxes

13 What is meant by the incidence of taxation?

A How the tax burden is shared between consumers and producers

B The extent to which tax is evaded

C What proportion of the country's products are taxed

D Who receives the tax revenue raised

14 What is meant by a regressive tax?

    A One designed to create a more even distribution of income

    B One which is impossible to evade

    C One which is earning less tax revenue than previously

    D One which takes a larger percentage of tax from the poor than the rich

15 A government wants to reduce income inequality. Which tax should it increase?

    A Excise duties

    B Import duties

    C Income tax

    D Sales tax

16 What is a disadvantage of a progressive system of income tax?

    A It discourages the growth of the informal economy

    B It may increase the mobility of labour

    C It redistributes income from the poor to the rich

    D It may act as a disincentive to work

17 Which feature is a quality of a good tax?

    A Convenience

    B Divisibility

    C Durability

    D Homogeneity

18 What would be an argument for removing a sales tax on food?

    A To decrease total (aggregate) demand

    B To decrease income inequality

    C To increase disposable income

    D To increase the tax base

19 What effect would an increase in labour productivity have on an economy?

    A A decrease in total (aggregate) demand

    B A decrease in the rate of economic growth

    C An increase in total (aggregate) supply

    D An increase in the labour force

20 A government increases its spending on benefits for the poor and raises the top rates of direct taxes. What does this suggest is its main aim?

    A Balance of payments stability

    B Economic growth

    C Price stability

    D Redistribution of income

21 A government wants to reduce unemployment and to reduce a deficit on the current account of the balance of payments. Which policy measure would be the most appropriate?

    A An increase in corporation tax

    B An increase in government spending on training

    C An increase in the rate of interest

    D A revaluation of the exchange rate

22 Why may full employment and price stability conflict as government aims?

    A Full employment may benefit from a fall in the exchange rate whereas price stability may benefit from a rise in the exchange rate

    B Full employment may benefit from an increase in aggregate supply whereas price stability may benefit from a decrease in aggregate supply

    C To achieve full employment may require a decrease in aggregate demand whereas to achieve price stability may require an increase in aggregate demand

    D To achieve full employment may require an increase in the rate of interest whereas price stability may require a decrease in the rate of interest

23 A government wants to encourage firms to expand production. Which combination of policy measures may achieve this objective?

	Corporation tax	Income tax
A	decrease	decrease
B	decrease	increase
C	increase	increase
D	increase	decrease

24 What does a consumer prices index show?

    A How the price of domestically produced products has changed over time

    B How the price of a representative basket of goods and services has changed over time

    C How the wages of consumers have changed relative to the change in the price level

    D How the wages of consumers have changed relative to the costs of production

25 A country is experiencing a high rate of inflation. Which item would be the least desirable store of wealth?

    A Money

    B Property

    C Land

    D Shares

26 In which circumstance would an increase in total (aggregate) demand be most likely to cause inflation?

    A It is caused by an increase in investment undertaken by expanding industries

    B It is the result of higher government spending on training which raises labour productivity

    C It occurs when there is a low level of spare capacity in the economy

    D It takes place when there is net immigration occurring

27 What is a cause of cost-push inflation?

    A A reduction in direct taxes

    B A reduction in the rate of interest

    C An increase in bank lending

    D An increase in the price of raw materials

28 What is a cause of demand-pull inflation?

    A A fall in labour productivity

    B A fall in investment

    C A rise in the budget deficit

    D A rise in a current account deficit

29 In which circumstance would a rise in a country's inflation rate increase the international competitiveness of the products it produces?

    A The quality of the products produced by other countries improves at a more rapid rate

    B The price level of other countries increases at a more rapid rate

    C The country's exchange rate increases

    D The productivity of the country's labour force decreases

30 Which group is economically active?

    A Full-time students

    B Those who are too sick to work

    C Those who are officially classified as unemployed

    D Those who have retired early

31 What is the cause of frictional unemployment?

    A A lack of total demand

    B The introduction of new technology

    C A lack of information about job vacancies

    D Domestic consumers buying more imports

32 Which factor may cause official unemployment figures to understate the actual level of unemployment?

    A People being ashamed to admit they are unemployed

    B People being prepared to cheat the system

    C People who have found employment since the measure was taken

    D People working in the informal economy

33 What type of unemployment is caused by workers changing jobs?

    A Cyclical

    B Frictional

    C Regional

    D Structural

34 An increase in which variable may cause unemployment?

   A Bank lending

   B Disposable income

   C Government spending

   D Imports

35 Why might a fall in unemployment increase the inflation rate?

   A It will increase total (aggregate) demand

   B It will increase total (aggregate) supply

   C It will reduce workers' wages

   D It will reduce the economy's productive capacity

36 Which government measure would be most effective in reducing structural unemployment?

   A Increasing government spending on training

   B Increasing the rates of unemployment benefit

   C Reducing income tax

   D Reducing the rate of interest

37 Which of the following payments would be included in the measurement of Gross Domestic Product?

   A Payments to those in the informal sector

   B Retirement pensions

   C Salaries of government ministers

   D Unemployment benefit

38 Which combination of changes may enable an economy to grow despite a rise in unemployment?

	Occupational mobility	Productivity
A	decrease	decrease
B	decrease	increase
C	increase	increase
D	increase	decrease

39 What is a possible disadvantage of economic growth?

   A Environmental improvement

   B Extra consumer goods produced

   C Higher tax revenue

   D Structural unemployment

40 Which method is one of the ways of measuring GDP?

   A The consumption method

   B The expenditure method

   C The import method

   D The payment method

41 How is a consumer prices index calculated?

    A By adding up the price changes of a basket of products

    B By attaching weights to a basket of products

    C By dividing price changes of a basket of products

    D By multiplying weights by the price changes of a basket of products

42 A country experiences inflation, but its citizens experience a rise in their purchasing power. Which change could explain this?

    A The exchange rate depreciating

    B The money supply increasing by more than output

    C Tax bands rising by more than inflation

    D Wages rising by more than prices

43 Which changes may result in sustained economic growth?

	Total (aggregate) demand	Total (aggregate) supply
A	decrease	decrease
B	decrease	increase
C	increase	increase
D	increase	decrease

44 What is meant by deflation?

    A A fall in the exchange rate

    B A fall in the price level

    C Negative economic growth

    D Negative net investment

45 Which changes to debt and the value of money are the consequences of deflation?

	Debt	Value of money
A	decrease	decrease
B	decrease	increase
C	increase	increase
D	increase	decrease

Part 7 Similarities and differences

Similarities

Find **one** similarity between each of the following pairs. Your answer to 6 should be helped by the work you did in answer to the questions on drawing diagrams.

1 Price stability and low inflation.

2 Economic growth and redistribution of income.

3 Fiscal policy and monetary policy.

4 Changes in the rate of interest and changes in the money supply.

5 Income tax and corporation tax.

6 The impact of an indirect tax on a product with inelastic demand and the granting of a subsidy on a product with inelastic demand.

7 Convenience and economy.

8 Increase in government spending and a decrease in the rate of interest.

9 Reforming trade unions and privatisation.

10 Tariffs and taxes on demerit goods.

11 Budgetary policy and fiscal policy.

12 Menu costs and shoe leather costs.

13 Claimant count and labour force survey.

14 Borrowers and workers with strong bargaining power.

15 Search unemployment and seasonal unemployment.

16 Lost output and lost tax revenue.

17 Income method and expenditure method.

18 Rise in quantity of resources and rise in quality of resources.

19 Pensions and unemployment benefits.

20 Nominal GDP and GDP at current prices.

Differences

Identify **one** way in which the two terms in each pair is different. You will note that question 7 includes the same terms (fiscal policy and monetary policy) as question 3 in the similarities section, but this time you are seeking to identify **one** way in which fiscal policy differs from monetary policy.

1 Employment and unemployment.

2 Deflation and a reduction in the inflation rate.

3 Budget position and the balance of payments.

4 Macroeconomic policies and microeconomic policies.

5 Actual economic growth and potential economic growth.

6 Progressive taxes and regressive taxes.

7 Fiscal policy and monetary policy.

8 Subsidies and taxes.

9 Income tax and inheritance tax.

10 Direct taxes and indirect taxes.

11 Cost-push inflation and monetary inflation.

12 Budget deficit and budget surplus.

13 Private sector employment and public sector employment.

14 The labour force participation rate and the employment rate.

15 Structural unemployment and cyclical unemployment.

16 Employed and self-employed.

17 Demand-side deflation and supply-side deflation.

18 Cost of living and standard of living.

19 Economic growth and recession.

20 Labour market reforms and a change in the money supply.

Part 8 Data response questions

Study the source material carefully for each question, then answer Questions 1 to 6.

Source material: South African unemployment

Unemployment has been a major problem in South Africa for some time. In 2016, a year when the country's real GDP rose by only 1% from $350 billion to $353.5 billion, there were 5.72 million unemployed workers in the country. The unemployment rate in that year, 26%, was slightly higher than in previous years. Figure 4.3 shows South Africa's unemployment rate between 2010 and 2016.

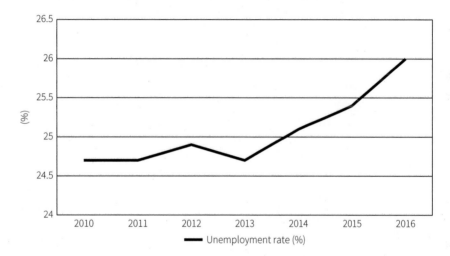

Figure 4.3: South Africa's unemployment rate, 2010–2016

Poor educational attainment in the country means there is a mismatch between unemployed workers and job vacancies. Many of the unemployed lack the skills required. This problem has been made worse by periods when total demand for goods and services in the economy has fallen. Some people who lose their jobs due to a lack of total demand, lose confidence and their skills become out of date. These two effects reduce their chances of gaining another job.

The existence of unemployment keeps tax revenue below what it could be. South Africa has a progressive income tax system. It is now possible for taxpayers to submit their tax forms online.

The South African government is using a range of policies to reduce unemployment which, in turn, it hopes will increase economic growth. In 2016, it increased its spending on education and on subsidies for newly recruited workers aged between 18 and 29. Table 4.2 shows how total government spending has changed over the period 2010 to 2016.

Table 4.2: % change in South African government spending

Year	%
2010	2.3
2011	3.0
2012	3.5
2013	2.0
2014	1.8
2015	0.3
2016	0.5

Some economists expressed concern that if the government were to raise its spending by more there would be the risk that the inflation rate could go even higher than the 6.6% rate experienced in 2016. The South African government has an inflation rate target of 3% to 6%.

1 Referring to the source material in your responses, answer all parts of Question 1.

   a Identify South Africa's economic growth rate in 2016. [1]

   b Calculate the size of South Africa's unemployment rate in 2016. [2]

> **TIP**
> Remember the formula for the unemployment rate.

   c Explain a government aim, other than full employment and economic growth. [2]

   d Explain **two** principles of taxation. [4]

   e Analyse the relationship between government spending and the unemployment rate. [4]

> **TIP**
> This is quite demanding as you have to use two pieces of data. Look carefully at the vertical axis in Figure 4.3.

   f Analyse the causes of unemployment in South Africa. [5]

   g Discuss whether or not a reduction in unemployment will cause economic growth. [6]

   h Discuss whether or not supply-side policy measures are always successful in reducing unemployment. [6]

> **TIP**
> The question mentions 'measures' in the plural so you need to discuss at least two measures.

Source material: State intervention in the Brazilian economy

Brazil did enjoy a period of high economic growth during which unemployment fell and investment rose. The destruction of the Amazon rainforest increased as there was more logging and more land taken to be used as farmland.

In 2010, the economy grew by 7.5%. It then fell and in 2015 it contracted by 3.8%. The recession continued into 2016 when output fell by 3.6%. The decline in economic activity had an impact on the government's tax revenue and its budget position. In 2016, the government's revenue was $632 billion and it had a budget deficit of $44 billion.

Some economists think that the government is imposing a considerable amount of regulation on the country's firms. The average firm spends more than 2000 hours a year to process its taxes. They think that it imposes a relatively high tax burden on its households and firms. In 2016, Brazilian tax revenue was equivalent to 31% of GDP. This compared with 21% in Chile and 19% in Mexico. The high level of taxation and regulation may be discouraging investment.

The Brazilian government spends the tax revenue on three main items. One is generous pensions for Brazilian government workers. Another is public sector workers' pay and the third is on transfers to the regional authorities of the country's 27 states which spend the money mainly on health, education and administration.

Public sector workers, on average, earn more than twice as much as workers in the private sector and have better working conditions. Most of those receiving the country's national minimum wage are private sector workers. Changes in wages can affect poverty and unemployment. Figure 4.4 shows Brazil's unemployment rate and the change in the average wage rate between 2010 and 2016.

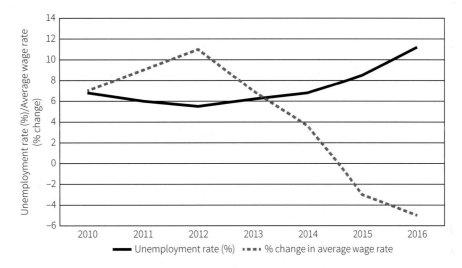

Figure 4.4: Brazil's unemployment rate and percentage change in average wage rate, 2010–2016

2 Referring to the source material in your responses, answer all parts of Question 2.

    a Identify a cost of economic growth. **[1]**

    b Calculate Brazil's government spending in 2016. **[2]**

    c Explain **one** way in which taxes place a burden on Brazilian firms. **[2]**

    d Explain **two** reasons why a Brazilian may prefer to work for the government rather than a private sector firm. **[4]**

    e Analyse the relationship between the unemployment rate and the change in the average wage rate in Brazil between 2010 and 2016. **[4]**

    f Analyse why a government may impose a national minimum wage. **[5]**

    g Discuss whether or not an increase in government spending on education would increase a budget deficit. **[6]**

    h Discuss whether or not the Brazilian government should cut taxes. **[6]**

TIP

There is more information in the extract to draw on to inform your answer here, but do not restrict your comments just to the current Brazilian situation.

Source material: Inflation in the UAE

The United Arab Emirates (UAE) government has used a range of policy measures to stop inflation rising to high levels. At the end of 2010, it announced plans to build up strategic stockpiles of essential foodstuffs to slow down inflation. It also considered imposing price controls on food sold in the country's shops. Another measure, under review at the time, was subsidising essential foodstuffs for its citizens.

At the start of 2016 the consumer prices index (CPI) in the UAE was 105. By the end of 2015 it had risen to 106.89. It was forecast that the inflation rate would rise between 2016 and 2020. Higher fuel prices were expected to affect, for example, transportation and electricity prices. It was also known that the planned introduction of value added tax (VAT) in January 2018 would have an impact on the price level. The effect of the tax on the demand for individual products would, of course, be influenced by their price elasticity of demand.

Forecasts were more uncertain as to what would be happening to the money supply in the future. Figure 4.5 shows how the money supply changed over the period 2012 to 2015 and the country's inflation rate.

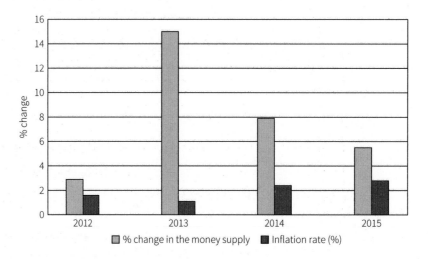

Figure 4.5: Percentage changes in the money supply and the inflation rate in the UAE, 2012–2015

The rise in prices in the UAE has affected the international competitiveness of the country's products. It has also influenced saving in the country with the rate of interest not always keeping pace with the inflation rate.

It is thought that consumer expenditure has been affected more by changes in the country's unemployment rate. The UAE has traditionally had a very low unemployment rate, but it rose to an annual average of 3.8% between 2012 and 2016. Although this rate was still low by international standards, it was thought the rise from previous years had slowed down the rise in consumer expenditure. The International Monetary Fund (IMF) was urging the UAE to cut government spending. Increases in government spending can cause inflation.

3   Referring to the source material in your responses, answer all parts of Question 3.

   a   Identify a component of total (aggregate) demand.   **[1]**

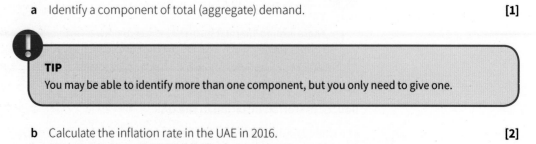

> **!**
>
> **TIP**
> You may be able to identify more than one component, but you only need to give one.

   b   Calculate the inflation rate in the UAE in 2016.   **[2]**

   c   Explain whether the inflation that the UAE was predicted to experience between 2012 and 2016, was demand-pull inflation or cost-push inflation.   **[2]**

   d   Explain **two** costs of inflation.   **[4]**

   e   Analyse the relationship between changes in the money supply and the inflation rate.   **[4]**

f Analyse, using a demand and supply diagram, the effect of imposing a maximum price on food. **[5]**

g Discuss whether or not an increase in government spending will cause inflation. **[6]**

h Discuss whether or not inflation is more harmful than deflation. **[6]**

Source material: The challenges facing the Philippines

In 2016, the government of the Philippines had a budget deficit of $7 billion. Its revenue, including revenue from corporation tax, income tax and value added tax (VAT), was not sufficient to finance its spending. The government said it was planning to increase the budget deficit in 2017 to spend more on infrastructure and education. It wanted to do this to boost economic growth and reduce unemployment. Consumer spending was also continuing to rise in 2016. This was encouraged by a high level of consumer confidence. Indeed, in an international survey, consumer confidence in the Philippines was ranked second highest in the world. Average household disposable income in the Philippines in 2016 was $6000 with $5100 being spent and $900 being saved.

The amount earned by workers in 2016 varied between sectors. Wages were higher in the tertiary and manufacturing sectors than in the primary sector. The proportion of workers employed in the primary sector was declining, but it was still relatively high at 28%. The proportion of workers in the public sector was also declining.

Inflation in the Philippines has fluctuated. One influence on changes in the price is bank lending. In 2016 lending by the country's commercial banks increased by 14% with a relatively high proportion of loans being taken out to finance the purchase of cars. The central bank of the Philippines uses changes in the rate of interest to influence both economic growth and the inflation rate. A fall in the rate of interest may be welcomed by consumers and producers, but it may increase inflationary pressure.

Figure 4.6 shows the relationship between the inflation rate and the interest rate in six countries in 2016.

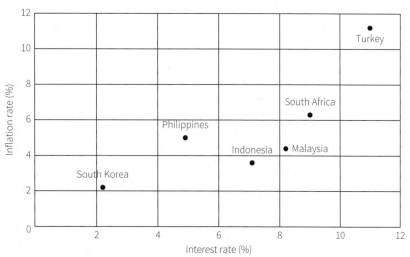

Figure 4.6: The relationship between the inflation rate and the interest rate in six countries in 2016

4 Referring to the source material in your responses, answer all parts of Question 4.

a Identify an example of an indirect tax. **[1]**

b Calculate the savings ratio in the Philippines in 2016. **[2]**

c Explain **one** cause of an increase in the money supply. **[2]**

d Explain how the pattern of employment in the Philippines has changed in recent years. **[4]**

e   Analyse **two** influences on consumption.   [4]

f   Analyse the relationship between the inflation rate and the interest rate in the countries shown.   [5]

TIP
Figure 4.6 is a scatter diagram. In assessing whether such a diagram shows a relationship, it is useful to consider whether there is a line of best fit.

g   Discuss whether or not an increase in consumption will always benefit an economy.   [6]

h   Discuss whether or not monetary policy or supply-side policy measures would be more effective in increasing economic growth.   [6]

Source material: Spain coming out of a recession for the second time

Spain experienced a recession which started at the end of 2008 and lasted until 2010. It went back into recession in 2012 and 2013. It returned again to positive economic growth in 2014, although it took one more year for the country's inflation rate to become positive again.

The government took a number of measures to boost output during these periods, but its membership of the single currency, the euro, prevented it from being able to use devaluation of the foreign exchange rate. With more people being out of work, the government also lost tax revenue to spend on expansionary policy measures.

During the two periods of recession, some Spanish banks got into trouble. A number of borrowers found they were unable to repay their loans. This made the banks more reluctant to lend. This reduced the growth in Spanish consumer expenditure and investment. The boom in housebuilding was also stopped.

The recent recovery of the Spanish economy has been driven largely by increases in consumer expenditure. In 2015, the Spanish government cut income tax rates twice. The higher level of economic activity has had an impact on the country's unemployment rate, as shown in Table 4.3.

Table 4.3: Economic growth rate and unemployment rate in Spain, 2012–2016

Year	Economic growth rate (%)	Unemployment rate (%)
2012	−3.0	25.1
2013	−1.8	26.3
2014	1.4	24.4
2015	3.2	22.1
2016	3.0	18.0

Spain's recovery has influenced the performance of neighbouring countries. For example, the unemployment rate in Portugal fell from 15.1% in 2013 to 10.2% in 2016. Some economists expressed concern that Spain's improved economic performance could result in Spain and its trading partners experiencing higher rates of inflation.

5   Referring to the source material in your responses, answer all parts of Question 5.

a   Identify a monetary policy measure.   [1]

b   Calculate the difference between Spain's and Portugal's employment rate in 2016.   [2]

TIP
Read this question carefully.

c Explain **one** cost of unemployment. [4]

d Explain **two** consequences of a recession. [4]

> **TIP**
>
> It is relatively easy to find one consequence mentioned in the extract. It takes a little more attention to find the second consequence.

e Analyse the relationship between economic growth and unemployment. [4]

f Analyse how housebuilding and economic growth are related. [5]

g Discuss whether or not the policy aims of economic growth and inflation will conflict in the case of Spain. [6]

h Discuss whether or not a cut in tax rates would increase economic growth. [6]

Source material: Changes in Chile's economic performance

Chile had a relatively high unemployment rate in 2012. There had been a reduction in government spending which had a knock-on effect on spending in the private sector. Investment was also declining. The economy was not booming.

The unemployment rate then fell until 2015. The strong labour market had an effect on wages and the country's output. It also had an impact on government spending on healthcare and on the inflation rate. Figure 4.7 shows Chile's unemployment rate and inflation rate in the period 2012–2016.

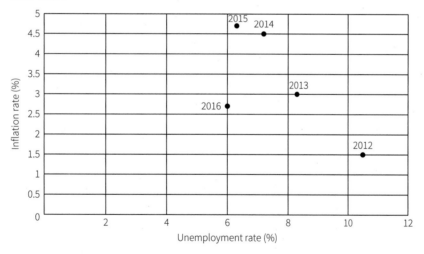

Figure 4.7: Unemployment and inflation rate in Chile, 2012–2016

The Chilean government thought the country's economic performance would be improved by attracting more investment from other countries. In this period, the USA was the largest investor in the country, particularly in its energy sector. To encourage more investment from the USA and other countries, the government was planning to cut taxes and improve education and healthcare. Some Chilean politicians opposed tax cuts, arguing they would reduce the government's tax revenue.

Despite the challenges facing the Chilean economy, it was claimed by some Chilean politicians that the economy was performing better than other Latin American countries including Argentina, Mexico and Venezuela. Table 4.4 shows some data on the four countries.

Table 4.4: Selected data on selected Latin American countries (2016)

Country	Economic growth rate (%)	Inflation rate (%)	Unemployment rate (%)
Argentina	−2.3	18.4	7.2
Chile	1.7	2.7	6.0
Mexico	1.1	4.8	4.1
Venezuela	−9.0	530.0	7.3

6 Referring to the source material in your responses, answer all parts of Question 6.

    a Identify the type of unemployment experienced by Chile in 2012. **[1]**

    b Explain what is likely to have happened to wages in Chile in the period 2013–2015. **[2]**

    c Explain what is meant by 'a booming economy'. **[2]**

    d Explain **two** effects, other than a change in wages and the inflation rate, of a fall in unemployment. **[4]**

    e Analyse the relationship between Chile's unemployment rate and the inflation rate. **[4]**

    f Analyse how a government could attract investment from abroad. **[5]**

    g Discuss whether or not a cut in taxes will lower tax revenue. **[6]**

    h Discuss whether or not the Chilean economy was performing better than the other economies shown in Table 4.4. **[6]**

Part 9 Four-part questions

1 The Chinese government is considering changing the balance between direct taxes and indirect taxes. In deciding which taxes to use, governments take into account the qualities of a good tax.

    a Define *income tax.* **[2]**

    b Explain the difference between a progressive and a regressive tax. **[4]**

    c Analyse the qualities of a good tax. **[6]**

    d Discuss whether or not a government should shift the burden of taxation from direct taxes to indirect taxes. **[8]**

2 Switzerland has traditionally come close to full employment. In contrast, South Africa has had high unemployment for some time. The South African government has been trying for some time to reduce unemployment in the country.

    a Define *full employment.* **[2]**

> **TIP**
> The stem, that is the information that introduces the question, might help you here.

    b Explain **two** government macroeconomic aims, apart from full employment. **[4]**

    c Analyse what may happen to unemployment if investment increases. **[6]**

    d Discuss whether or not the unemployment of labour is more serious than the unemployment of other factors of production. **[8]**

TIP
You may find it helpful to plan your answer before you start writing it.

3 Governments may use fiscal policy to reduce unemployment and so to reduce the disadvantages that unemployment can impose on an economy. Both fiscal policy and monetary policy seek to influence total demand.

    a Define *fiscal policy*. **[2]**

    b Explain **two** causes of unemployment. **[4]**

    c Analyse the disadvantages of unemployment to an economy. **[6]**

TIP
You may wish to highlight or underline 'disadvantages' in the question to remind you not to write about advantages. You might also want to highlight 'to an economy' so that you do not concentrate on the unemployed for example.

    d Discuss whether or not a rise in total demand will increase employment. **[8]**

4 Norway has had a relatively stable inflation rate in recent years. The country's government spends a higher proportion of its GDP, 7%, than the global average of 5%. It has increased its spending on infrastructure, including roads, railways and broadband connections. At the start of 2017 the government was planning to privatise much of the rail network.

TIP
This is a relatively long introduction to the question. It could help you in your answer to part **c** if you were uncertain about the meaning of infrastructure.

    a Define *a consumer prices index*. **[2]**

    b Explain why governments aim for a stable inflation rate. **[4]**

TIP
You may wish to highlight the word 'stable' here to ensure you focus on stable inflation.

    c Analyse how firms might benefit from an increase in government spending on education and infrastructure. **[6]**

    d Discuss whether or not an industry should be privatised. **[8]**

5 In 2016 Ethiopia had an economic growth rate of 9.8% and an inflation rate of 8.5%. In contrast, the USA had an economic growth rate of 1.6% and an inflation rate of 1.7%. Despite the difference in inflation rates, it was expected that the rate of interest would rise in both countries in 2017.

    a How is economic growth measured? **[2]**

    b Explain why a country can have a higher real GDP, but a worse economic growth performance than another country. **[4]**

    c   Analyse how an increase in the rate of interest would affect firms. **[6]**

    d   Discuss whether or not an economy experiencing 8.5% inflation would face more serious problems than one facing an inflation rate of 1.7%. **[8]**

6   The Cambodian economy has been growing relatively rapidly in recent years. Its growth rate has averaged 7%. Its consumer prices index in 2016 rose by 5%. In the same year, the official unemployment rate was the second lowest in the world at 0.5%.

    a   Identify **two** types of unemployment. **[2]**

    b   Explain how the basket of goods and services is used to calculate the consumer prices index. **[4]**

    c   Analyse how a government could reduce inflation. **[6]**

    d   Discuss whether or not economic growth is always desirable. **[8]**

Answering four-part question 2

Below is a sample answer to question 2. The answer contains some common weaknesses. Read each part and consider how the answer could be improved.

a Full employment is when the labour force is fully employed. There is zero unemployment.

b One government macroeconomic aim is low and stable inflation. Governments do not aim for zero inflation as measures of inflation tend to overstate price rises. A low inflation rate may encourage producers to make more. A stable rate makes it easier for firms and households to plan for the future.

     Another macroeconomic aim is for the economy to produce more. If an economy is making more goods and services, it will export more. The extra exports will increase the economy's revenue and more people can be employed producing them.

c If people save more in financial institutions, they will be spending less. This means that if investment increases, demand will fall. If demand is less, firms will lower their output. To produce less output, firms will need fewer workers. They may make some workers redundant. This type of unemployment is called cyclical unemployment and can be on a large scale.

d The unemployment of labour reduces the income the unemployed receive. The unemployment of other factors of production will reduce the income of those who own the other factors of production.

     The unemployment of workers can cause the workers' skills to become out of date so they will find it hard to be employed again. If capital goods are unemployed, they may also become out of date.

     If unemployed workers have less income, the unemployed may suffer worse health. They will not be able to spend as much on the education of their children and so their children may be unemployed in the future.

     Unemployment means resources are not being fully used. Output is less than it couldbe.

     The unemployment of labour reduces tax revenue and increases the cost of unemployment benefits. The unemployment of land and capital also reduces tax revenue, but does not result in higher benefits.

Unemployment of labour can lead to the unemployed being out of work for some time. Structural unemployment may arise as workers will miss out on training and keeping up to date with technological advances.

Improve the answer...

Here are some ways to improve the above answer. Did you think about these?

a The answer shows a common confusion. In economics, full employment is not taken to be zero unemployment.

b The first part of the answer is strong. It correctly identifies a macroeconomic aim and goes on to explain it. The second part, however, is not strong. It states that a macroeconomic aim is to achieve a higher output, but does not recognise that this is economic growth. The student also does not establish why exports would rise. Just because more products are made, does not mean that more will be exported. There has to be demand for the exports as well as potential supply.

c The answer shows an awareness of the link between a change in demand and a change in employment. Unfortunately, it makes a fundamental and common mistake at the start. This is a confusion over the meaning of investment. In economics, investment is spending on capital goods.

d There are some good points made in this answer. It should, however, have been more direct on whether the unemployment of labour is more serious than the unemployment of other factors of production. There are three direct comparisons between the unemployment of labour and the other factors of production. The first two occur in the first two paragraphs and the third in the second to last paragraph. There are, however, a number of places where the opportunity to make a comparison was missed. For instance: 'Unemployment means resources are not being fully used. Output is less than it could be.' In this case, it could have been mentioned that the unemployment of any factor of production will result in output being lower than its potential. After reading the answer, it is not certain whether the student thinks the unemployment is more serious or not as the relative impact on the different factors of production has not been brought out sufficiently.

The answer should also have been more clearly thought out and organised. It is rather disjointed. For example, lower income for workers is referred to in the first paragraph and then the student returns to this point again to develop in further in the third paragraph. It would have been better if the effect of lower income was considered in one paragraph.

Economic development

Learning summary

Before completing the activities in this section, review your work on these topics:

- Living standards
- Poverty
- Population
- Differences in economic development between countries

LINK

See Chapters 32–35 in the Coursebook.

Part 1 Definitions

Matching the definitions to the appropriate terms should help you distinguish between a number of similar terms.

Match the following terms with the appropriate definitions.

1	Economic development	**a**	Unrecorded economic activity
2	Dependency ratio	**b**	A diagram showing the age structure of a population
3	Birth rate	**c**	The average number of children born to each woman in the country
4	Human Development Index	**d**	How income is shared between households
5	Income inequality	**e**	Emigration of skilled workers
6	Distribution of wealth	**f**	The number of deaths per thousand live births
7	Absolute poverty	**g**	An improvement in people's lives including a rise in self-esteem
8	Relative poverty	**h**	The number of births in a year per thousand of the population
9	Income distribution	**i**	A measure of living standards which includes the components of education, health and living standards
10	Natural increase in population	**j**	A rise in the average age of the population
11	Net emigration	**k**	A situation where people lack the income to participate in the normal activities of the country
12	Population pyramid	**l**	A situation where people lack some of the basic necessities of life
13	Ageing population	**m**	Movement of people between countries and regions
14	Distribution of income	**n**	The number of deaths in a year per thousand of the population
15	Gender distribution	**o**	An uneven distribution of income between households

16 Fertility rate		**p**	The increase in population resulting from an excess of births over deaths
17 Optimum population		**q**	More people leaving the country than entering it
18 Migration		**r**	The percentage of the population who are not of working age
19 Brain drain		**s**	The quality of people's lives
20 Infant mortality rate		**t**	The difference between the number of people entering and leaving the country during a year per 1000 people
21 Death rate		**u**	How assets are shared out among households
22 Living standards		**v**	The ratio of males to females in the population
23 Informal economy		**w**	How income is spread between households
24 Gender distribution		**x**	The study of population
25 Net migration rate		**y**	The proportion of the population that are male and the proportion that are female
26 Demography		**z**	The size of population which gives the highest output per head

Part 2 Missing words

Fill in the missing words, taking particular care with 8, 11 and 19.

1 One country may have a higher real GDP per head than another country, but most of its citizens may experience lower _____ _____ if income is very _____ distributed.

2 A vicious circle of poverty can be present in developing countries with low saving leading to low _____ which in turn leads to low _____ which results in low _____.

3 A country may achieve economic growth without experiencing economic _____ if the choices facing people are _____ and the distribution of income becomes more _____.

4 A more uneven distribution of wealth would tend to lead to a more uneven distribution of _____, as wealth generates _____.

5 Cutting progressive taxes, charging for state education and abolishing a national _____ wage would make the distribution of _____ more _____.

6 A rise in the income of the poor is likely to reduce _____ poverty, but _____ poverty may increase if the income of the rich increases at a greater rate.

7 Governments reduce income inequality by transferring some _____ revenue to the _____.

8 The birth rate of a country is likely to be low if a _____ proportion of women go to university, a _____ of women work and it is _____ to bring up children.

9 Net immigration will tend to _____ the labour force of a country and reduce the _____ ratio as most immigrants are of working age.

10 The concept of _____ population compares population size and _____ per head.

85

11 A _____ in the infant mortality rate in a country may reduce the birth rate as it may encourage families to have _____ children.

12 An ageing population will _____ the dependency ratio and create a _____ demand for healthcare.

13 Net emigration would be disadvantageous if a country's population is _____ the optimum level.

14 A high level of international debt will be more difficult to repay if interest rates _____ and if the country's export revenue _____.

15 _____ substitution increases reliance on _____ production and reduces reliance on foreign production.

16 The United Nations and the _____ Bank provide _____ aid as opposed to bilateral aid.

17 The ownership of land is very unevenly distributed in Latin America. This inequality results in both _____ and _____ poverty.

18 Children of the poor tend to grow up poor as they usually have _____ years of education and _____ access to healthcare.

19 A triangular population pyramid shows a high birth rate and a _____ death rate and is more likely to be found in a _____ country than in a _____ country.

20 More money may flow from _____ countries to _____ countries if debt repayments are greater than foreign aid.

Part 3 Calculations

Question 1 here tests your understanding of 'a natural increase in population' and question 3 requires you to know what is meant by 'cumulative percentage'. Be careful with question 2 – check what it is asking.

1 A country starts the year with a population of 120 million. By the end of the year 2 million children have been born, 500 000 people have died and there has been net emigration of 500 000. What was the natural increase in population?

2 A country has a population of 30 million, 80% of whom live above the level of absolute poverty. How many of its people are living in absolute poverty?

3 From Table 5.1 below, calculate the cumulative percentage of income.

Table 5.1

Group	% share of income
Poorest 20%	7
Next poorest 20%	11
Middle 20%	18
Next richest 20%	22
Richest 20%	42

Part 4 Interpreting diagrams

1 Using Figure 5.1 below, explain two reasons why Country B is likely to be a more developed economy than Country A.

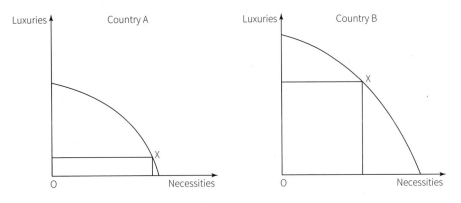

Figure 5.1

Part 5 Drawing diagrams

Using a production possibility diagram in each case, illustrate the effect of:

a   emigration of workers

b   an increase in investment

c   an improvement in healthcare

Part 6 Multiple choice questions

Read the options carefully as in a number of cases they are very similar.

1   Which change could cause a natural decrease in population?

  A   A fall in the death rate
  B   A fall in the birth rate
  C   Net emigration
  D   Net immigration

2   What is meant by 'absolute poverty'?

  A   An income level that is insufficient to meet basic needs
  B   An income level that is less than 25% of the national average
  C   A lack of any income
  D   A lack of any wealth

3 What may promote both economic growth and economic development?

    A   A more uneven distribution of income

    B   Improved education of the poor

    C   Increased output of heavy polluting firms

    D   Increased tax on company profits

4 What is meant by the 'optimum population'?

    A   A population which produces the highest output per head

    B   A population with an equal number of males and females

    C   A population which is static

    D   A population with a low average age

5 What is meant by the term 'overpopulation'?

    A   There is a high geographical density of population

    B   There is a high population relative to the available area of cultivatable land

    C   There is a high population relative to the economic resources available

    D   There is net immigration

6 What impact would economic development have on adult illiteracy, infant mortality and life expectancy?

	Adult illiteracy	Infant mortality	Life expectancy
A	reduce	reduce	increase
B	increase	reduce	reduce
C	increase	increase	reduce
D	reduce	increase	increase

7 Two countries have the same size of population. One country has a lower number of hospital beds per 100 000 people, but is considered to have a better standard of healthcare. What could explain this?

    A   Life expectancy is lower in this country

    B   Patients are treated more efficiently in this country

    C   This country has fewer doctors per 100 000 people

    D   This country is more prone to infectious diseases

8 What would indicate that a country is experiencing economic development?

    A   A fall in its death rate

    B   A fall in its savings rate

    C   A rise in its economic inactivity rate

    D   A rise in its malnutrition rate

9 As an economy develops, what usually happens to the population of workers employed in the primary and tertiary sectors?

	Primary	Tertiary
A	decrease	decrease
B	decrease	increase
C	increase	increase
D	increase	decrease

10 Which of the following may be a barrier to economic growth?

   A A reluctance to lower the school leaving age

   B A resistance to change

   C A high level of investment

   D A high level of productivity

11 How is healthcare measured in the HDI?

   A Doctors per head of population

   B Government spending on healthcare

   C Hospital waiting lists

   D Life expectancy

12 A country has a lower real GDP per head than another country but also a smaller percentage of people living in absolute poverty. What could explain this?

   A The country has a lower rate of inflation

   B The country has a lower population

   C The country has a more even distribution of income

   D The country has more people employed in the primary sector

13 What tends to happen to a country's birth rate and death rate as it develops?

	Birth rate	Death rate
A	decrease	decrease
B	decrease	increase
C	increase	increase
D	increase	decrease

14 Which of the following may increase the birth rate in a country?

   A Improved healthcare

   B A rise in the school leaving age

   C Reduced job opportunities for women

   D The introduction of a generous state pension scheme

15 Which activity by a US multinational company with a branch in the Philippines may increase the economic development of the Philippines?

   A The payment of wages at a lower rate than in the USA, but at a higher rate than in the Philippines

   B The pressure on the government of the Philippines to cut its spending on healthcare

   C The purchase of imported raw materials from the USA

   D The transfer of profits back to the USA

16 Which form of foreign aid is most likely to be successful in promoting economic development?

    A Tied, bilateral aid

    B Tied, multilateral aid

    C Untied, bilateral aid

    D Untied, multilateral aid

17 What is meant by a country's population growth?

    A The difference between a country's birth rate and death rate plus immigration

    B The difference between a country's birth rate and death rate plus net migration

    C The increase in a country's population in a year expressed as a percentage of the working population at the beginning of the year

    D The increase in a country's population expressed as a percentage of world population at the beginning of the year

18 What could lead to a virtuous circle?

    A Low savings

    B Low tax revenue

    C High imports

    D High productivity

19 A country has a low real GDP per head. What must this mean?

    A Everyone in the country is poor

    B Government spending on welfare benefits is high

    C On average income levels are low

    D There are no millionaires living in the country

20 What would increase the ratio of males to females in a country?

    A A fall in the death rate of males

    B A reduction in the infanticide of female babies

    C A rise in the emigration of males

    D A rise in the immigration of females

21 Why might a poor developing country experience net immigration?

    A It has a high and rising unemployment rate

    B It has a low and declining real GDP per head

    C It is surrounded by poorer countries

    D It is surrounded by countries with more lenient immigration controls

22 Why may a rich developed country have a declining labour force?

    A It may have experienced a falling birth rate

    B It may have experienced a falling death rate

    C It may have experienced net immigration

    D It may have reduced the retirement age

23 Which policy measure would increase absolute and relative poverty?

    A A cut in state benefits

    B A cut in indirect taxes

    C An increase in government spending on state education

    D An increase in government spending on state healthcare

24 A country has low GDP per head, low productivity, a high level of international debt and is experiencing a natural increase in population. Which feature may be found in such a country?

    A A death rate which is exceeding the birth rate

    B A net inflow of interest payments on past debts

    C High output per worker hour

    D Some households with high levels of income

25 A country experiences a fall in its HDI despite a rise in life expectancy. What could explain this?

    A A fall in access to clean water

    B A fall in mean years of education

    C A rise in air pollution

    D A rise in gender inequality

Part 7 Similarities and differences

Similarities

Identify **one** way in which each pair is similar. You may have to spend a little longer on some of these, for example 4, 7 and 8, than on others.

1   Real GDP per head and the Human Development Index.

2   Birth rate and death rate.

3   A low level of savings and poor infrastructure.

4   A national minimum wage and generous state benefits.

5   Emigration and immigration.

6   Low wages and unemployment.

7   Rise in birth rate and fall in death rate.

8   Rise in the dependency ratio and increase in the cost of state pensions.

9   International debt and reliance on primary products.

10 Unemployment and old age.

Differences

Identify **one** way in which each pair differs.

1   Economic growth and economic development.

2   Human Development Index and Multidimensional Poverty Index.

3   Natural change in population and migration.

4   Emigration and immigration.

5 Economic growth and population growth.

6 Import substitution and export promotion.

7 Vicious circle and virtuous circle.

8 Distribution of income and distribution of wealth.

9 Overpopulated and underpopulated.

10 Growing population and ageing population.

Part 8 Data response questions

Study the source material carefully for each question, then answer Questions 1 to 4.

Source material: Income distribution in Brazil

Income is very unevenly distributed in Brazil. In 2014, the country recorded the fourth most uneven distribution in the world. Table 5.2 shows how income was distributed in Brazil in 2014.

Table 5.2: Income distribution in Brazil, 2014

Share of	% of income
Lowest 20%	3.6
Second 20%	7.9
Third 20%	12.6
Fourth 20%	19.6
Richest 20%	?

It has been estimated that in 2015 20% of the country's population lived in poverty with 3.5% living in extreme poverty, lacking the resources to meet basic human needs, including minimum nutrition needs and adequate medical treatment.

One of the main policy measures the Brazilian government uses to reduce poverty is its Bolsa Familia (Family Scholarship) scheme. This was introduced in 2003 and in 2014 it reached 13.8 million families. It requires parents to keep their children in school and take them to clinics for health check-ups and have them vaccinated against common diseases. It is designed to break the cycle of poverty by ensuring that children are healthier and better educated than their parents. Reductions in poverty and income inequality can affect adult literacy. Figure 5.2 shows the Gini coefficient, a measure of inequality (the higher the figure, the greater the inequality), and adult literacy rates for a number of countries.

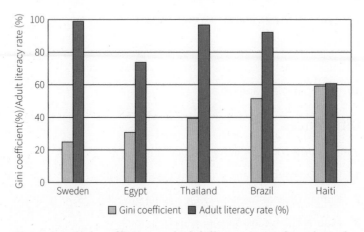

Figure 5.2: Gini coefficient and adult literacy rates for selected countries, 2014

The government has increased its spending on education, particularly primary school education, and has operated a national minimum wage since 1940. It is providing agricultural training, financial incentives, water cisterns and, in some cases, houses for people living in rural areas. It is hoped that these measures may help to reduce not only poverty, but also some of the problems caused by the rural to urban migration in the country. The movement of people from the countryside to towns and cities can put pressure on housing and there is no guarantee that the migrants will find employment.

The government has had some success in reducing income inequality. It has been calculated that between 2003 and 2014, 29 million people were lifted out of poverty and that the country's Gini coefficient had fallen from 58.1 to 51.5. This reduction in poverty and inequality was, however, halted in 2015 and 2016 when the country experienced a recession.

1 Referring to the source material in your responses, answer all parts of Question 1.

    a Identify what type of poverty is referred to. **[1]**

    b Calculate the share of Brazil's total income received by the richest 20% in 2014. **[2]**

    c Explain why a recession may increase poverty. **[2]**

> **TIP**
> This is a question which could be explored in depth, but the number of marks indicates you should keep your answer brief.

    d Explain **two** possible problems of rural to urban migration. **[4]**

    e Analyse how improved healthcare can break the cycle of poverty. **[4]**

    f Analyse the relationship between inequality of income and literacy rates. **[5]**

    g Discuss whether or not the Brazilian government should spend more on education. **[6]**

    h Discuss whether or not a government should try to reduce income inequality. **[6]**

Source material: The importance of remittances

Some people choose to work abroad to take advantage of greater employment and training opportunities and higher pay. It is becoming increasingly easy for workers to send money back home to their relatives. Remittances is the term given to money sent by migrant workers, people working in another country, to their relatives in their home country.

Remittances are an important source of income in some economies. Indeed, in a number of economies, more money is now coming from remittances than from foreign aid, foreign investment or even traditional exports. In 2016, migrant workers sent back $602 billion which was more than double the figure for 2006. In that year, the Philippines received the third highest value in remittances behind India and China.

Remittances are particularly important for the Philippines. In 2016, they accounted for $30 billion, 10.2% of the country's GDP. Filipinos work as domestic helpers, sailors, labourers, factory workers and nurses throughout the world. The top destinations of all migrant workers are the USA, Saudi Arabia and Germany. In the case of the Philippines, the top destination is Saudi Arabia. Table 5.3 shows both the number of overseas Filipino workers (OFWs) and the country's unemployment rate.

Table 5.3: The unemployment rate in the Philippines and the number of overseas Filipino workers (OFWs), 2010–2015

Year	Unemployment rate (%)	Number of OFWs (millions)
2010	7.3	1.47
2011	7.0	1.69
2012	7.0	1.80
2013	7.1	1.84
2014	6.8	1.85
2015	6.3	2.20

Losing workers to other countries has both advantages and disadvantages. It can result in skill shortages and training can be wasted. For example, Jamaica has to train five and Grenada twenty-two doctors to keep just one. The remittances can also push up the exchange rate which makes the country's exports more expensive and can discourage investment which may reduce the country's development.

On the other hand, they can reduce poverty. For example, some of the money sent back may be used to educate the children of those who are working abroad. Remittances are also more reliable than foreign direct investment, fluctuating to a much lesser extent.

2 Referring to the source material in your responses, answer all parts of Question 2.

  a Identify **one** source of foreign currency available to the Philippines. [1]

  b Calculate the GDP of the Philippines in 2016. [2]

  c Explain what evidence there is that training is a merit good. [2]

  d Explain **two** reasons, other than higher employment opportunities, why someone from the Philippines may go abroad to work. [4]

  e Analyse the relationship between the unemployment rate in the Philippines and the number of overseas Filipino workers. [4]

  f Analyse how investment can promote development. [5]

TIP
Make sure you write about 'investment' in its economic sense.

  g Discuss whether or not the emigration of workers from a country promotes the development of that country. [6]

  h Discuss whether or not the growth of the Saudi Arabian economy will promote economic growth in the Philippines. [6]

TIP
You do not need any specific knowledge of the two economies other than that given in the extract.

Source material: Japan's falling population

In 2016 Japan had a population of 126 million, but its population was ageing and declining at such a rate that some economists were predicting that there would be only one Japanese person by 3000!

Changes in a country's population size can influence its output which, in turn, can influence living standards and the cost of living. Figure 5.3 shows Japan's population growth rate and its economic growth rate in recent years.

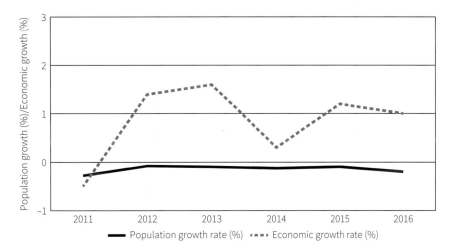

Figure 5.3: Japan's population growth rate and economic growth rate, 2011–2016

In 1947 5% of Japan's population was aged over 65, by 2008 this had risen to 20% and by 2016 it had increased to 27%. At the moment, there are four Japanese workers for every retired person. This will be two to one by 2030 and three to two by 2050. The rise in the proportion of older people is putting an increasing burden on the country's healthcare system.

The Japanese government is seeking to offset the effects of an ageing population by encouraging more mothers to enter the labour force and by raising the retirement age. A higher retirement age increases the size of the labour force and reduces the cost of state pensions. In 2016, the retirement age was increased from 61 to 62 and it will be increased to 65 by 2025.

The Japanese population is ageing because of a fall in the death rate and birth rate. In 1947 Japanese life expectancy was 50. This had increased to 84 by 2016. The fertility rate fell below the replacement rate of 2.1 in the early 1970s and was as low as 1.4 in 2016. In that year, the country's birth rate was 7.8 and its death rate was 9.5.

3 Referring to the source material in your responses, answer all parts of Question 3.

    a Identify a cause of a decline in population. **[1]**

    b Calculate the natural increase in Japan's population size in 2016. **[2]**

    c Explain what is likely to be happening to Japan's dependency ratio. **[2]**

    d Explain **two** effects of an ageing population. **[4]**

    e Analyse the relationship between Japan's population growth rate and economic growth rate over the period shown. **[4]**

    f Analyse **two** ways of measuring living standards. **[5]**

TIP

Select the two you feel most confident analysing. Your ability to analyse two methods is what is important here, not your ability to identify two obscure methods.

    g Discuss whether or not an increase in the cost of living will reduce people's living standards. **[6]**

    h Discuss whether or not a declining population is beneficial. **[6]**

95

Source material: Water – the development issue of the 21st century

One of the United Nations' Sustainable Development Goals (SDGs) is to ensure universal access to safe and affordable drinking water and sanitation for all by 2030. It was estimated that out of a world population of approximately 7.5 billion in 2017 about 2.1 billion people did not have access to safe water and 650 million were without basic sanitation.

The basic water requirement per person per day is 50 litres although, for a short time, it is possible to get by on 30 litres. Whilst the average US citizen uses 500 litres per day and UK citizens 200 litres a day, in a number of countries people have to try to survive on less than 10 litres each. For example, in Mozambique it is 9.3 litres, Somalia 8.9 litres, Mali 8 litres and Gambia it is as low as 4.5 litres per person.

Table 5.4 shows how access to clean drinking water and other influences on the quality of lives differs between a number of countries.

Table 5.4: Factors influencing the quality of life in selected countries, 2016

Country	% of population with access to safe drinking water	GDP per head ($s)	Doctors per 1000 people	Average years of schooling	Cars per 1000 people	Life expectancy at birth (years)
Angola	49	3360	0.08	5.2	2	53.1
Cuba	95	7650	5.90	11.8	38	79.8
Kuwait	99	27 100	1.53	7.5	530	75.0
Nepal	92	740	0.21	4.1	5	70.0
Singapore	100	54 500	1.42	15.4	152	83.5
South Africa	93	5200	0.77	10.4	166	57.6

Water is used not just for drinking, washing and disposing of human waste, but also by industry and agriculture. Indeed, it takes 1400 litres to produce a kilo of maize and a staggering 42 500 litres to produce a kilo of beef.

Whilst two-thirds of the earth is made up of water, 97.5% of this is salt water. The remaining 2.5% of the useable freshwater is available in lakes, rivers, groundwater and rainfall runoff. The increasing shortage of this water is resulting in deaths and diseases. For example, it has been estimated that one out of every five deaths of children under five is due to water-related diseases. One child dies from dehydration caused by diarrhoea every 14 seconds and half of the world's hospital beds are taken up with people with water-borne diseases. It is also resulting in international disputes. There are conflicts between Botswana, Namibia and Angola over the water in the Okavango Basin and between Egypt, Sudan and Ethiopia over the water in the Nile.

It has been estimated that the money needed to meet the SDGs on water and sanitation is $20 billion. This is a small proportion of the $130 billion that is spent in the west on bottled water and could significantly reduce the death rate caused by lack of access to safe drinking water.

Aid to improve access to safe water and sanitation has actually declined in recent years and, in addition, a higher proportion is now given in loans rather than grants which is pushing indebted countries further in debt.

4 Referring to the source material in your responses, answer all parts of Question 4.

    a Identify a possible opportunity cost of using water for drinking. **[1]**

    b Calculate what proportion of the world's population was without access to clean water in 2017. **[2]**

TIP
This is a straightforward question.

c Explain whether water is evenly distributed. [2]

d Explain what is likely to happen to demand for water in the future. [4]

e Explain how lack of water hinders development. [4]

f Analyse how the quality of life varied between the countries in 2016. [5]

TIP

There is a considerable amount that you could write here, but remember that this question only carries 5 marks. You need to be selective. Avoid simply repeating what is in the table. For example, writing that Angola has 47% of its population without access to safe drinking water and a GDP per head of $3360 is not analysis. It does not involve any processing of the information.

g Discuss whether or not high income countries should provide grants to low income countries to improve the supply of their water. [6]

h Discuss whether or not a country will benefit from a fall in its death rate. [6]

Part 9 Four-part questions

1 Governments seek to achieve economic growth and economic development. For example, Malawi's Growth and Development Strategy sees economic growth as the key to poverty reduction and improvement in living standards. Some governments think that rapid economic growth will bring about more economic development.

a Define *economic development*. [2]

b Explain **two** reasons why a government may want to see a reduction in absolute poverty. [4]

c Analyse why all economies are seeking to become more developed. [6]

d Discuss whether or not rapid economic growth always results in more economic development. [8]

TIP

Make sure you focus on *rapid* economic growth.

2 The USA has a high real GDP per head, but also an uneven distribution of income. Rwanda has a significantly lower real GDP per head, but a much more even distribution of income.

a Explain what is meant by an 'uneven distribution of income'. [2]

b Explain how the levels of absolute and relative poverty are likely to differ in a low income country with an even distribution of income and a high income country with an uneven distribution of income. [4]

c Analyse how a government can influence the distribution of income. [6]

d Discuss whether or not allowing more immigration would benefit a rich country. [8]

TIP

See answering four-part questions below.

3 It was estimated that in 2016, 20 million people in Russia were living below the country's poverty line of $139 a month. The Russian government was aiming to reduce poverty and to increase the population size as it was predicted the country would lose 20% of its population by 2050.

    a Define *a poverty line*. **[2]**

    b Explain **two** causes of an increase in the size of a country's population. **[4]**

    c Analyse **three** ways a government could influence the size of population. **[6]**

    d Discuss whether or not an increase in the size of population will be beneficial for an economy. **[8]**

4 India's death rate is declining and it is predicted that it will be the most populous country by 2050 at 1.6 billion. The country's government is currently seeking to increase literacy, particularly female literacy. It is also running the country's space programme.

    a Identify **two** causes of a fall in the death rate. **[2]**

    b Explain why the growth of a country's population may be lower than predicted. **[4]**

    c Analyse the benefits of educating girls. **[6]**

> **TIP**
> Stay objective. Avoid uninformed statements based on personal opinions such as 'girls are brighter than boys' and 'there is no point educating girls'.

    d Discuss whether or not a space programme will promote economic growth. **[8]**

Answering four-part question 2

Below is a sample answer to question 2. The answer contains some common weaknesses. Read each part and consider how the answer could be improved.

a An uneven distribution of income is when income is unevenly distributed.

b Absolute poverty will be higher in a low income country. There will be a greater proportion of people living on a low income not being able to afford e.g. adequate housing. People in the low income country will also be poor relative to the people in the high income country.

c A government could redistribute income by taxing the rich more and giving some of the tax revenue to the poor. This should make the rich less rich and the poor less poor. If the poor are less poor they should be healthier and more productive. This may increase tax revenue and employment. Redistributing income from the rich to the poor may be thought to be unfair. The rich may have worked hard to earn a high income. Taxing them more may mean they will be discouraged from working hard.

d A rich country should not allow more immigration. If more people come into the country, the wage rate will be reduced and unemployment will be increased. More unemployment will reduce a country's output. It will lower tax revenue and so the government will be able to spend less on education and healthcare which could reduce living standards.

With more people being out of work, there will be less demand for firms' products. Firms' profits will fall and they may be discouraged from investing. But they will find it easier to employ more workers if they do want to expand.

Those who are unemployed are likely to have less income. This may affect their health if now they cannot afford nutritious food and good housing. Their children may not get a good education. They may stay unemployed for a long time.

A rich country should allow more immigration. The rise in unemployment will reduce total demand. The lower demand will reduce inflation. Lower prices will enable people to buy more.

Improve the answer...

Here are some ways to improve the above answer. Did you think about these?

a The student here has just rearranged the words. It is difficult to state what is meant by the term without using the same words, but an example here would help to bring out the meaning.

b The student started well, explaining how absolute poverty would be likely to vary between the two types of countries. The second sentence also brings out the meaning of absolute poverty although a little more detail would have been useful. The third sentence, however, shows that the student has not read the question carefully enough. She has not taken into account the reference to the distribution of income in the two types of countries which might have helped her bring out an accurate understanding of relative poverty. Time has to be taken here to think out the answer before you start writing it. If you consider the question carefully, you should be able to answer it clearly and concisely.

c This is not a strong answer. It is vague at the start. There a number of ways a government could influence the distribution of income. These should be analysed in some depth. The student then wastes time and effort by seeking to evaluate whether a government should try to redistribute income. This is not what the question is asking.

d Again, this is not a strong answer. The student started by asserting that immigration would reduce the wage rate and increase unemployment. She needed to establish why this might be the case. The student then just concentrated on the effects of an increase in unemployment. Indeed, what the student appears to have done is something that a number of students do, that is to turn the question into a question they would like to answer.

In the last paragraph, the student also shows some confused thinking. A reduction in inflation is not the same as lower prices. Prices would still be rising and the unemployed would have less income to spend.
The student needed to examine more of the possible effects that immigration might have and to establish the points made.

Learning summary

Before completing the activities in this section, review your work on these topics:

- International specialisation
- Free trade and protection
- Foreign exchange rates
- Current account of the balance of payments

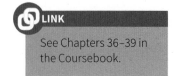

LINK

See Chapters 36–39 in the Coursebook.

Part 1 Definitions

Some of the definitions here are relatively long. Match each with the appropriate term, ensuring that all twenty fit.

1	Trade in services	**a**	Selling a product in a foreign market below cost price
2	Primary income	**b**	The ability of a country's firms to sell their products abroad
3	International trade	**c**	Speculative flows of money around the world taking advantage of changes in interest rates and exchange rates
4	Trade restrictions	**d**	A rise in the value of one currency relative to another due to market forces
5	Import expenditure	**e**	A fall in the free market value of a currency in terms of other currencies
6	Strategic industry	**f**	An action by the government or central bank to reduce the value of a currency under a system of fixed exchange rates
7	Dumping	**g**	An exchange rate that is determined by market forces
8	The exchange rate	**h**	International trade conducted without any government interference
9	A floating exchange rate	**i**	A declining industry
10	Depreciation	**j**	Receipts and payments of investment income
11	Devaluation	**k**	A newly established industry
12	Appreciation	**l**	Measures designed to protect domestic industries from foreign competition
13	Sunset industry	**m**	Bans on the trade in particular products or with particular countries
14	Hot money flows	**n**	Limits on the quantity of a product that can be traded
15	International competitiveness	**o**	An industry that is considered to play an important role in the economy

16	Free trade	p	The volume of imports multiplied by the price of imports
17	Protectionism	q	Trade in items such as banking and insurance
18	Quotas	r	The exchange of products between individuals and firms in different countries
19	Embargoes	s	Restrictions on the exchange of products across national borders
20	Infant industry	t	The price of one currency in terms of another

Part 2 Missing words

There are a number of sentences here which have only one word missing. Nevertheless, each sentence requires careful thought.

1   The four parts of the _____ account of the balance of payments are trade in _____, trade in, _____, primary income and secondary income.

2   If a German firm buys raw materials from a Namibian firm this will appear as a _____ item in the _____ account of Namibia's balance of payments.

3   International trade enables firms to take greater advantage of economies of _____, but changes in _____ rates may affect the revenue they receive from selling their products.

4   A country's firms are likely to export more if the country's inflation rate _____ and the productivity of workers _____.

5   A current account deficit on the balance of payments may be mainly a cyclical or a structural deficit. A _____ deficit is more serious.

6   A possible benefit of an increasing current account deficit on the balance of payments is a fall in the _____ rate.

7   Higher world output, but increased interdependency, arises from countries _____.

8   Two countries can both benefit from engaging in _____ trade even if one country has an _____ advantage in producing both products provided there is a difference in countries' _____ advantage.

9   A rise in a country's inflation rate may lead to a fall in its _____ rate and a deterioration in its trade in _____ and services.

10 A rise in a country's _____ rate will increase _____ prices, but reduce _____ prices.

11 A government or central bank may raise the value of its currency by increasing the country's _____ _____ or buying its _____.

12 The value of a floating exchange rate may rise if speculators believe the price of the currency will _____ in the near future and if there is net foreign _____ investment.

13 Hot money flows will be attracted into a country by a rise in the _____ _____ or an expectation that the exchange rate will _____.

101

14 An increase in income tax may decrease a current account _____ by reducing consumer spending on _____.

15 A _____ economic growth rate and a _____ share of world trade may indicate that a country's international competitiveness is declining.

16 A government may discourage imports by imposing _____ on a range of products. These are taxes on imports and are designed to make imports more expensive relative to _____ produced products.

17 Protectionism would be reduced by removing exchange _____ and reducing the _____ standards that imports have to meet.

18 The key argument for protecting sunset industries is to prevent an increase in _____. Over time, however, workers who retire or leave to take up employment in other industries will not be _____.

19 A country's workers may receive low wages, but its products will not be internationally _____ if its workers have _____ productivity.

20 The removal of trade restrictions may benefit consumers by increasing _____ and lowering _____.

Part 3 Calculations

1 Table 6.1 shows the output of wheat and tractors in Country X and Country Y.

Table 6.1: Output of wheat and tractors

	Output per worker per day	
	Wheat (tonnes)	**Tractors**
Country X	25	5
Country Y	75	10

  a Which country has the absolute advantage in producing wheat?

  b What is the opportunity cost of producing tractors in both countries?

  c Which country has the comparative advantage in producing tractors?

2 The Kenyan exchange rate changes from 70 Kenyan shillings (KSh) equals $1 to 100 KSh equals $1. What will be the resulting change in the US price of a 210KSh Kenyan export and the Kenyan price of a $20 US import?

Part 4 Interpreting diagrams

In analysing the causes and consequences of exchange rate changes, it is very helpful to use demand and supply diagrams.

1 a Identify two possible causes of the change in the value of the pound sterling shown in Figure 6.1.

  b Describe what effect the change shown is likely to have on the UK's trade in goods and services balance.

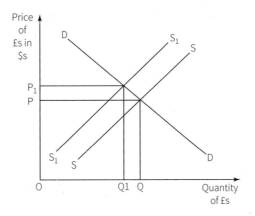

Figure 6.1: The market for £s

Part 5 Drawing diagrams

Use an exchange rate diagram in each case to illustrate the effect on the value of the Pakistani rupee of:

a   A rise in the value of Pakistani exports

b   Speculation that the value of the Pakistani rupee will fall

c   Pakistani firms buying out firms in India.

Part 6 Multiple choice questions

1   Which change would increase international trade?

    A   An increase in the difference in production costs between countries

    B   An increase in the difference in health and safety regulations between countries

    C   A rise in tariffs

    D   A rise in transport costs

2   Which of the following is an item that would appear in the trade in services component of the balance of payments?

    A   Books

    B   Paper

    C   Printing presses

    D   Royalty payments

3   What would increase the debits on a country's balance of trade in goods and services?

    A   Domestic firms buy more imported raw materials

    B   Domestic insurance companies sell more policies to foreign residents

    C   A foreign firm investing in the country

    D   The government receiving a loan from a foreign bank

4 Which section appears in the current account of the balance of payments?

A Capital

B Financial

C Net errors and omissions

D Primary income

5 Which change may reduce a country's current account deficit?

A An increase in the country's rate of inflation

B An increase in the quality of imports

C A rise in incomes abroad

D A rise in the exchange rate

6 To increase world output, on what cost should countries base their specialisation on?

A Average

B Fixed

C Opportunity

D Variable

7 A country has a comparative advantage in producing paper. What must this mean?

A The country produces more paper than any other country

B The country produces more paper than any other product

C The opportunity cost of producing paper in the country is lower than in other countries

D The resources used to produce it are not available in other countries

8 Two countries are considering trading cars and TV programmes. The output per worker of these products in the two countries is shown in the table.

Output per worker per month		
	Cars	TV programmes
Country X	20	60
Country Y	40	120

What can be concluded from this information?

A Trade will benefit Country X only

B Trade will benefit Country Y only

C Trade will benefit both countries

D Trade will not benefit either country

9 A country has a comparative advantage in producing sugar. Its government decides, however, to discourage its producers from specialising in sugar production. What could explain this decision?

A The country lacks an absolute advantage in sugar production

B There is an absence of foreign tariffs on sugar production

C The government wants a diversified industrial structure

D The government believes the productivity of workers in the domestic sugar production industry is increasing

10 A fall in the exchange rate reduces a current account deficit. What could explain this?

    A Export prices falling by less than export volume rises

    B Export prices rising by more than export volume falls

    C Import prices rising and import volume remaining unchanged

    D Import prices rising by more than import volume falls

11 What determines the value of a fixed exchange rate, but not of a freely floating exchange rate?

    A Export revenue and import expenditure

    B Foreign direct investment

    C Government intervention in the foreign exchange market

    D Speculation

12 Which change would cause the value of the US dollar to rise?

    A US interest rates rising

    B US firms buying firms in foreign countries

    C US tourists spending more abroad

    D US inflation rate rising more rapidly than other countries' inflation rates

13 The UK pound falls in value against the US dollar from £1:$2 to £1:$1.8. What will be the effect of this change?

    A Dollars will become more expensive in terms of pounds

    B Fewer pounds will be exchanged for a given number of dollars

    C UK imports from the USA will become cheaper

    D US imports from the UK will become more expensive

14 What is meant by dumping?

    A The employment of cheap labour

    B The imposition of tariffs on imports

    C The removal of health and safety standards

    D The sale of products below cost price in another country

15 What may cause a country's export prices to rise relative to its import prices?

    A A fall in the country's costs of production

    B Would reduce export prices and raise import prices

    C Would be likely to reduce export prices

    D may cause demand for imports to rise which would cause import prices to rise

16 Which of the following would cause a rise in Japan's exports of services to Malaysia?

    A Japanese airlines carrying more Malaysian passengers

    B Malaysian firms buying more ships from Japan

    C More Japanese tourists visiting Malaysia

    D More Malaysians travelling on Japanese built trains in Malaysia

17 Which change would increase the level of protection to domestic industries?

    A A reduction in income tax

    B A reduction in quota levels

    C A reduction in subsidies to domestic producers

    D A reduction in tariffs

18 The Vietnamese government decides to increase tariffs on imported buses. Which two groups in Vietnam may benefit from this decision?

    A Bus travel companies and bus passengers

    B Bus producing companies and bus travel companies

    C Bus passengers and the government

    D The government and bus producing companies

19 What is a valid argument for protectionism?

    A To correct a long-standing current account deficit

    B To increase the choice available for consumers

    C To prevent dumping driving out domestic producers

    D To protect employment overseas

20 Which item would be included in the current account position of South Africa's balance of payments?

    A The granting of a loan to a South African firm from an Italian bank

    B The payment of dividends to foreigners owning shares in South African countries

    C The purchase of a hotel in Madagascar by a South African citizen

    D The sale of a wildlife park to a US company

Part 7 Similarities and differences

When considering a similarity or a difference between the two terms in each pair, remember to do this in an international context.

Similarities

1 Exports and imports.

2 Trade in services and invisible balance.

3 Trade in goods and trade in services.

4 Inflation rate and exchange rate.

5 Revaluation and appreciation of the exchange rate.

6 Current account deficit and current account surplus

7 Speculation and foreign direct investment.

8 Voluntary export restrictions and quality standards.

9 Strategic industries and infant industries.

10 Less choice and retaliation.

Differences

Remember, what you are looking for here is differences in the meaning of the two terms in each pair.

1 Trade in goods balance and current account of the balance of payments.
2 Trade in goods surplus and trade in goods deficit.
3 Internal trade and international trade.
4 A cyclical current account deficit and a structural current account deficit.
5 Devaluation and depreciation of the exchange rate.
6 A fixed exchange rate and a floating exchange rate.
7 Free trade and trade protection.
8 Sunrise industries and sunset industries.
9 Hot money flows and foreign direct investment.
10 Credit items and debit items.

Part 8 Data response questions

Study the source material for each question carefully, then answer Questions 1 to 4.

Source material: The rise of the US dollar

Starting in the middle of 2014, the US dollar experienced a rapid appreciation against the euro, the currency used by most members of the European Union. By 2016, it took only $1.1 to buy 1 euro and so 1 euro could only buy $1.1. Table 6.2 shows how the euro to dollar exchange rate and the deficit on the current account of the US balance of payments has changed in recent years.

Table 6.2: The euro to US dollar exchange rate and current account deficit, 2010–2016

Year	Price of euros in US dollars	Current account deficit (US$bn)
2010	1.34	−382
2011	1.39	−430
2012	1.29	−442
2013	1.34	−365
2014	1.33	−391
2015	1.21	−463
2016	1.10	−481

The US central bank, the Federal Reserve, increased the country's interest rate in 2015 and 2016. In contrast, the European central bank reduced the rate of interest. Confidence in the US economy grew in this period, while it fell in the economy of the European Union. This affected the demand for the two currencies.

In 2016, Americans consumed $502 billion more in goods and services than the country produced. In that year, US exports of goods and services fell to $2209 billion which some American economists predicted would increase unemployment in the country.

The current account balance of the USA is influenced by changes in the economies of the USA and its trading partners. The effect of these changes is not always certain. For example, a more rapid rate of US economic growth may increase or reduce its exports. A fall in the exchange rate of another currency against the US dollar, caused perhaps by the sale of its currency, would affect the price of the USA's exports and imports.

1 Referring to the source material in your responses, answer all parts of Question 1.

    a Identify **one** way other than changing the interest rate in which a central bank could influence the value of the country's currency. **[1]**

    b Calculate the value of US imports of goods and services in 2016. **[2]**

> **TIP**
>
> The information is there in the source material, but you have to interpret the information.

    c Explain why a more rapid rate of economic growth may cause a fall in exports. **[2]**

    d Explain how 'less confidence in the European Union' could raise the value of the US dollar. **[4]**

    e Analyse how a decrease in exports may increase unemployment. **[4]**

    f Analyse the relationship between the change in the value of the US dollar and the deficit on the current account of the US balance of payments. **[5]**

> **TIP**
>
> Take care in interpreting the changes in the exchange rate. Apart from the table, there is some other information in the source material to help you.

    g Discuss whether or not a fall in the value of a country's exports will cause a current account deficit. **[6]**

    h Discuss whether or not a country will benefit from a fall in the value of its currency. **[6]**

Source material: China threatens to retaliate against US tariffs

In 2016, the USA had a deficit on the current account of its balance of payments whereas China had a current account surplus. In January 2017, the USA imposed a tariff of 52.5% on Chinese exports of washing machines. A month later the US government took action to reduce imports of steel products from China. It imposed tariffs ranging from 64% to 190% on Chinese steel products.

The US government claimed its trade restriction on Chinese steel products was justified on grounds of taking measures to discourage dumping, selling steel products at a lower price than at home. The US government also claimed that China was subsidising its steel products, making them artificially cheap.

The Chinese government argued that the help it was giving to steel producers was not excessive and that the US government had failed to show the extent to which it helped its exporters. It also threatened to impose import duties on US products in retaliation.

In recent years, China has been selling more exports to more markets throughout the world. Figure 6.2 shows the destination of Chinese exports in 2016.

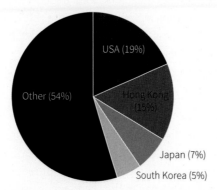

Figure 6.2: Share of Chinese exports, 2016

China's costs of production are relatively low. In 2016, it had a similar inflation rate as that of the USA, but the US government claimed that the Chinese central government was keeping the Chinese foreign exchange rate artificially low.

2 Referring to the source material in your responses, answer all parts of Question 2.

a Identify **one** motive for imposing tariffs. **[1]**

b Explain why China was so concerned about the USA imposing tariffs on its exports. **[2]**

c Explain what is meant by exports being 'artificially cheap'. **[2]**

d Explain why if a country's firms produce a product at a lower cost than firms in rival countries, they may not always sell more. **[4]**

> **TIP**
> You may want to highlight the word 'not' here.

e Analyse, using a demand and supply diagram, how the sale of its currency by its central bank could influence its foreign exchange rate. **[4]**

f Analyse what factors could explain why the USA had a current account deficit in 2016, while China had a current account surplus in 2016. **[5]**

g Discuss whether or not a government should retaliate when another country's government imposes tariffs on its exports. **[6]**

h Discuss whether or not a government should aim for a current account surplus. **[6]**

Source material: Indian spice exports

India accounts for approximately 45% of the global spice exports, even though only a small proportion, approximately 8%, of its annual production is traded internationally. Other major producers of spices are China, Pakistan and Vietnam.

In 2015 and 2016, a range of factors helped to push up demand for India's spices. These included increased incomes in Europe and the USA and an increased reputation for quality. Producing and exporting more spices can help to reduce unemployment and improve the country's balance of payments position.

Chilli is the most important spice in India's spice exports. In 2015, the value of Indian exports of chilli rose by 8% in value terms. India's exports of pepper also rose. This was partly because of concerns about pest contamination of Vietnam's crop. Vietnam is the world's largest producer of pepper. In 2015, the country produced 34% of the world's supply of pepper. In an average year, it exports 95% of its crop. The harvest in Vietnam is, however, often affected by changes in weather.

Vietnam is diversifying its economy. In recent years, the country has experienced rapid economic growth. The quality of the lives of its inhabitants is improving, with children receiving more education and healthcare improving. Average life expectancy is increasing in the country. In 2016, it was higher than India's and Pakistan's, but below that of China.

As a result of the rising demand for spices, both Vietnamese and Indian farmers were considering producing more species. Indian farmers were planning to devote more resources to growing crops not only of pepper and chilli, but also garlic, ginger, turmeric and mint. They were concerned, however, about the volatility of global prices and the unpredictability of the weather.

India exports and imports a range of products throughout the world. Figure 6.3 shows the destination of India's exports and the source of India's imports in 2015.

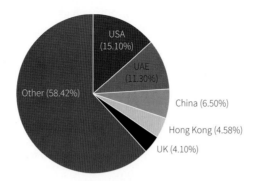

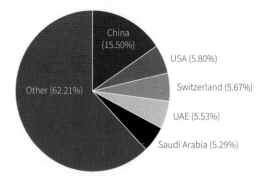

Figure 6.3a: Destination of India's exports, 2015

Figure 6.3b: Source of India's imports, 2015

3 Referring to the source material in your responses, answer all parts of Question 3.

a Identify **one** reason why demand for Indian spices increased. **[1]**

b Explain what evidence there is to suggest that India has the capacity to increase its exports of spices. **[2]**

c Explain the impact that an increase in the sales of spices would have on the current account of India's balance of payments. **[2]**

d Explain **two** reasons why a country's inhabitants may have a higher average life expectancy than the inhabitants of another country. **[4]**

e Analyse how the destination of India's exports compares with the sources of its imports. **[4]**

f Analyse, using a demand and supply diagram, the impact on the market for Indian pepper of a good harvest in Vietnam. **[5]**

g Discuss whether or not a rise in imports is always a disadvantage for a country. **[6]**

h Discuss whether or not Indian farmers should devote more resources to growing spices. **[6]**

Source material: International competitiveness and tourism

International competitiveness can be defined as the ability of a country's firms to compete successfully in international markets and so allow the country to continue to grow. Sometimes economists interpret international competitiveness narrowly in terms of price competitiveness. However, it is more usually taken to also include competitiveness in terms of quality and marketing.

There is a wide range of factors that influence an economy's international competitiveness. These include transport infrastructure, productivity, education and training and innovation.

Cuba and Bangladesh in 2016 were seeking to make their tourism industry more internationally competitive. Cuba's tourism industry accounts for 10% of its GDP and is a crucial earner of foreign exchange. The main visitors to the country are Canadians. The country was pressing for the US government to lift its embargo on US citizens visiting the country as tourists. It was also trying to boost tourist numbers from other countries by, for example, building more hotels and golf courses across the country.

The tourism industry is less developed in Bangladesh, accounting for 4.5% of the country's GDP in 2016. The government and the private sector are seeking to increase the size of the industry in a variety of ways. These include training more staff for the tourism industry and improving the country's infrastructure to make travel around the country easier. A number of foreign-owned hotels, including the US-owned Best Western hotel chain, are now operating in the country.

There is increasing competition throughout the world both for tourists and for foreign investment. To attract tourists, hotels have to charge competitive prices. In 2016, one hotel in Dhaka, the capital of Bangladesh, was charging 7650 taka for a night's stay. At this time, the exchange rate was $1 = 85 taka. Governments were competing for foreign investment in a number of ways, including changing the rate of corporation tax.

Tourism can have a noticeable effect on the current account balance of the balance of payments. Figure 6.4 shows how the current account balance of Bangladesh and three other Asian countries changed between 2010 and 2016.

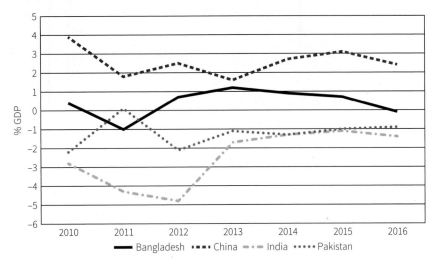

Figure 6.4: Current account balance as a percentage of GDP of four countries, 2010–2016

Becoming more internationally competitive is not all beneficial. For example, if the firms in an economy become more competitive, this is likely to push up the country's foreign exchange rate.

4   Referring to the source material in your responses, answer all parts of Question 4.

   a   Identify **one** method of protection.   [1]
   b   Calculate the price in US dollars of a night's stay in Dhaka in 2016.   [2]
   c   Explain **one** factor that could attract foreign direct investment to a country.   [2]
   d   Explain how international competitiveness and the exchange rate are linked.   [4]
   e   Analyse the current account balance of the four countries shown.   [4]
   f   Analyse how a government could make the country's tourism industry more
       internationally competitive.   [5]
   g   Discuss whether or not a government should protect an infant industry.   [6]
   h   Discuss whether or not a firm will benefit from producing in more than one country.   [6]

Part 9 Four-part questions

1 Globalisation is presenting both opportunities and challenges for countries. Changes in the global economy is one reason why the balance on the current account of Nigeria's balance of payment went from a surplus to a deficit in 2015. This change, which continued in 2016, and influenced the value of the naira, Nigeria's currency.

   a   Define *globalisation*.   [2]
   b   Explain **two** of the components of the current account of the balance of payments.   [4]

> **TIP**
> Select the two components that you will feel most confident writing about.

c Analyse the consequences of a current account deficit. **[6]**

d Discuss whether or not a fall in the exchange rate will always improve the trade in goods position. **[8]**

2 The International Monetary Fund, a global organisation, promotes the benefits of free international trade and opposes protectionism. It encourages member countries to remove tariffs and other trade restrictions. Countries can, however, influence their current account balances in other ways, including increasing income tax.

a Define *a tariff*. **[2]**

b Explain **two** benefits of free international trade. **[4]**

c Analyse two arguments for protectionism. **[6]**

d Discuss whether or not an increase in income tax would correct a deficit on the current account of the balance of payments. **[8]**

TIP
See answering four-part questions below.

3 Both Japan and the USA operate a floating exchange rate. Japan traditionally has had a trade in goods surplus, while the USA has had a trade in goods deficit. Changes in a country's foreign exchange rate can influence a country's economic performance.

a Define *a trade in goods deficit*. **[2]**

b Explain **two** benefits of a floating exchange rate. **[4]**

c Analyse the factors that could cause a rise in a country's exchange rate. **[6]**

d Discuss whether or not a rise in a country's exchange rate will help a government achieve its macroeconomic objectives. **[8]**

4 In 2016 Pakistan's economy was facing both a current account deficit and a budget deficit. Such deficits often result in a fall in the external value of the currency. A depreciation can cause an outflow of hot money and affect the profits earned by multinational companies.

a Define *hot money flows*. **[2]**

b Explain the difference between a current account deficit and a budget deficit. **[4]**

TIP
The introduction to the question should make clear to you that these are macro and not micro terms.

c Analyse the effect that a fall in the value of its currency is likely to have on a country's inflation rate. **[6]**

d Discuss whether or not a multinational company will maximise profits. **[8]**

Answering four-part question 2

Below is a sample answer to question 2. The answer contains some common weaknesses. Read each part and consider how the answer could be improved.

a A tariff is a tax on imports. The tariff will raise the costs of those selling imports. Some of this higher cost is likely to be passed on to consumers in the form of a higher price. The higher price will reduce the quantity demanded. Tariffs may be imposed to reduce imports or to raise revenue for the government. There is a risk that tariffs will not work if importers cut their prices or if demand is inelastic.

b Free international trade may result in some firms in the country going out of business. They may be undercut by more efficient foreign firms. This could increase unemployment. Free international trade means that a government cannot get revenue from tariffs. For some countries, tariff revenue is an important source of income.

c One argument would be to protect declining industries. This would stop unemployment occurring. Protectionism can stop dumping. Imports will no longer be able to be sold at a low price and so domestic firms will sell more. Protectionism can also help infant industries. Without protection, they will not be able to grow and the country's output will be lower.

d An increase in income tax could turn a current account deficit into a current account surplus. It would leave people with less to spend. They may buy fewer imports. A decrease in import expenditure will improve the trade in goods and services components of the current account balance.

Firms may try to sell more exports if they cannot sell all of their output in the domestic market. More exports would increase the chances of a current account being reduced. An increase in income tax would increase the government's tax revenue. The government could now spend more on training. This could make workers more productive. Rises in the quality and reductions in the costs and prices of goods and services produced would be likely to increase exports and reduce imports. An increase in income tax should correct a current account deficit.

Improve the answer...

Here are some ways to improve the above answer. Did you think about these?

a There is nothing wrong with what is written here, but the student has not made good use of his time. He has gone beyond defining the term. There would be no additional marks for this and the time and effort could have been spent more usefully on Q2(c) and Q2(d).

b The student has not read the question carefully enough. He has written about two potential costs rather than benefits.

c Here the student wrote about three arguments when only two were asked for. Even more significantly the student did not answer the question in sufficient depth. He jumped stages. For example, he did not establish why protecting declining industries would stop unemployment occurring and the link between dumping and low prices was not brought out.

d What there is of this answer is quite good. The problem is that it is one-sided. The student should also have considered why an increase in income tax may not correct a current account deficit.

113